THE GROWTH OF CANADIAN PAINTING

I. JAMES WILSON MORRICE, R.C.A. (1865-1924)
" Ice Bridge over the St. Lawrence "
Oil: $23\frac{1}{2}'' \times 31\frac{1}{2}''$.   *Montreal Museum of Fine Arts*

THE GROWTH OF CANADIAN PAINTING

BY

DONALD W. BUCHANAN

With a Foreword by
ERIC NEWTON

With 16 reproductions in colour and 64 in monochrome

COLLINS LONDON AND TORONTO

First Published 1950

PRINTED IN GREAT BRITAIN
TEXT AND COLOUR PLATES PRINTED AND THE BOOK BOUND BY
WILLIAM COLLINS SONS AND CO., LTD., GLASGOW
PHOTOGRAVURE SECTIONS PRINTED BY
THE VANDYCK PRINTERS LTD., BRISTOL
COLOUR BLOCKS BY THE SUN ENGRAVING CO., LTD., WATFORD
1950

AUTHOR'S PREFACE

In the following pages you will not find any orthodox history of Canadian art. What I have tried to give instead is a chart of twentieth-century painting in Canada in which I hope the more prominent figures will stand out clearly enough to allow the reader to understand the lie of the land. From James Wilson Morrice, who died in 1924, to Jack Nichols, who was born in 1921, my choice of artists covers several generations and a wide range of achievement. Something of the environment of Canadian culture, I should also like to think, has crept into these essays as well as some hint of that diversity of impulse and of experiment which marks the best of Canadian painting to-day.

An introductory chapter has been included on the earlier developments, in which landmarks of the nineteenth century are noted and in which the careers of a few artists, whose work serves as a transition between that era and more contemporary movements, are indicated briefly.

Three of these essays have appeared already in the magazine *Canadian Art*, of which Robert Ayre and I are the editors, and I have also revised for the purpose of publication here two or three articles which I wrote a few years ago for the *Canadian Geographical Journal*. My thanks go to Andrew Bell and Jacques de Tonnancour and Robert Ayre for allowing me to quote a number of extracts from contributions of theirs to *Canadian Art*, and to Kathleen Fenwick for her criticism and generous help in the final stages of the preparation of my manuscript. During the course of my studies, I made considerable use of the research facilities of The National Gallery of Canada, and of their photographic archives. The National Gallery also undertook the labour of bringing together and shipping on loan to the blockmakers in England the sixteen paintings which had been selected as being most suitable for reproduction in colour in this book. I am also grateful to other museums and to various private collectors for the permission they gave me to reproduce paintings owned by them. I have visited the studios of most of the men and women whose work is described in these pages. Many of them are my personal friends. Jack Humphrey I had, however, never met ; so I preferred that Graham McInnes, who knew his work more intimately, should contribute the essay on him.

My hope is not only that this book will serve to show how deep and genuine has been the growth of creative activity in Canadian painting but also that it may bring something of the flavour of Canada itself, the land and its culture, to readers in other countries.

D. W. B.

Ottawa, 1950

CONTENTS

COLOUR ILLUSTRATIONS

MONOCHROME ILLUSTRATIONS

FOREWORD

A FOREWORD to a book which already contains an author's preface is, at best, little more than a decorative headpiece. It can, and should, bestow a blessing and an air of importance on what follows, but whoever writes it must be careful of his words, for a blessing is apt to sound a little pompous and patronising, and an air of importance can only be bestowed by an authority.

None the less, though I am certainly not an authority on Canadian art, I do bestow a blessing on this book. It commends itself to me in two ways, the first of which is personal and private and therefore no concern of the reader : yet I insist on mentioning it since it gives me my only right to figure in these pages at all. I visited Canada in early 1937. I travelled from city to city ; I was welcomed with a warmth that still seems to me unbelievable and which I know was undeserved. Under the paternal guidance of Mr. Harry McCurry, now Director of the National Gallery of Canada, I lectured on art, I met a great many artists, I made friends with the author of this book, I marvelled at the vitality and enthusiasm I encountered and the oddly difficult conditions under which both flourished in the vast, beautiful, half-empty Dominion. I returned to England much wiser and in many respects humbler, and I still feel for Canada a nostalgia which has been intensified by reading this book. Any English reader who shares my initial admiration for Canadian art will find himself a victim of the same nostalgia. My personal blessing, therefore, is privately addressed to Mr. Buchanan for so effectively carrying me back over a gap of thirteen years.

But there is a second and a more important reason why I welcome the opportunity to pronounce a blessing. Nostalgia is a poignant and a not unpleasant emotion but it can only be felt at a distance. To Canadians this will not be a nostalgic book but a stimulating and a revealing one. Canada's art has now passed through all the recognised stages of babyhood, boyhood, adolescence, maturity—even the sowing of wild oats, that necessary prelude to maturity. It has established its right to a serious historian, and in Mr. Buchanan it has found the historian it deserves—a man familiar with the facts, yet by no means a chilly and indifferent statistician. Pride and affection, never boastful but, thank goodness, always biased, are implicit behind his steady flow of criticism and information. He is the kind of historian I like.

Much of his information—especially that contained in the earlier part of the book—was already known to me. In 1937 the Group of Seven had disintegrated as a unit, but their hard-won victories were, even then, only just being recognised throughout the length and breadth of Canada. They had, in fact, done something very unusual : they had founded a national and completely independent style. They had expressed the moods of Canadian landscape to Canadians as bravely as the artists of fifteenth-century Italy had expressed Renaissance culture to Italians. It was a magnificent achievement. Nor had the Group of Seven a monopoly. One of my vividest recollections is of meeting that solitary genius, Emily Carr, in Victoria and of spending two astonishing days in her studio surrounded by hundreds of her sketches and paintings of giant trees and virgin forests. The effect was of stumbling on a well-stocked library of books on a new theme and written in a new but easily legible language.

Since then a new generation has grown up. As this book brings the story of Canadian art nearer to our own day the information it contains becomes less familiar to me, the names of the artists less nostalgic, their work more scholarly and (dare I say it ?) less Canadian, more international.

Such a development was inevitable. The pioneer always has a more recognisable character than his more sophisticated successor. The violently changing moods of Canadian landscape are local. Nudes, still-lifes and formalised paintings are universal. Not that Paris and London have imposed their accents on Toronto and Montreal, but that early struggles through virgin undergrowth tend to produce individuals : later consolidations of the conquered ground produce types.

This pattern of the growth of a national art emerges clearly enough in Mr. Buchanan's book. He has been wise enough not to generalise too much. He leaves it to the reader to make his own generalisations. As he adds each short essay to the last, the separate links begin to form a connected chain, and anyone with eyes to see has only to refer to the plates in order to realise what a formidable chain it is.

ERIC NEWTON.

London, 1950.

1. PAUL KANE (1810-1871)
"Blackfoot Chief"
Oil: 30¼″ × 25″. Montreal Museum of Fine Arts

2. CORNELIUS KRIEGHOFF (1815-1872)
" Winter Landscape "
Oil: 38½″ × 51″.   *National Gallery of Canada, Ottawa*

3. UNKNOWN

" Fredericton, New Brunswick "

Oil: 18½″ × 26″.   *The William H. Coverdale Collection, Montreal*

4. ANTOINE-SÉBASTIEN PLAMONDON, R.C.A. (1804-1895)
"La Chasse aux Tourtes"
Oil: 72½″ × 72″. Art Gallery of Toronto

5. WILLIAM BRYMNER, R.C.A. (1855-1925)
"Woman Sewing"

Oil: 25½″ × 16″. *Montreal Museum of Fine Arts*

6. MAURICE CULLEN, R.C.A. (1866-1934)
" Shipyard, Lauzon, in Winter "
Oil: 21″ × 28¾″. François Dupré, Esq., Montreal

7.   HORATIO WALKER, R.C.A. (1858-1938)
"The Royal Mail"
Oil.   Private Collection

8. MARC-AURÈLE DE FOY SUZOR-COTÉ, R.C.A. (1869-1937)
" French Canadian Type "
Oil. Private Collection

EARLY GROWTH AND FIRST ACHIEVEMENTS

To THE question, who was the first Canadian painter, no simple and explicit answer can be given. Certainly one hesitates to grant this distinction to any of those early monks or abbés, whose religious portraits and votive offerings have come down to us from the French regime, for they were usually no more than dutiful amateurs. The one exception perhaps was Frère Luc ; he had been trained under Simon Vouet in France, but he only worked in Canada briefly during 1670-71.

Twenty years after the English conquest of New France, a Canadian, François Malepart de Beaucourt, who had been living in Europe, returned home and produced in this country a few paintings, one of which, *The Portrait of a Negro Slave*, now in the McCord Museum, Montreal, still retains some historical interest for us to-day. But his work apparently exerted little influence, for even after his death in 1794 no spark could yet be encountered of any native tradition in painting. Strangely enough, in the old ramparted town of Quebec, there arose instead about this time among both higher bourgeoisie and clergy alike a novel and curious passion for acquiring as many copies as possible of the works of the old masters, whether Flemish, Italian or French. Parallel to this, there developed among the young of talent a correspondingly strong urge to learn how to make presentable copies of copies. Several young men of promise went to Europe to perfect themselves in this craft. For example, Antoine Falardeau was presented with a scholarship raised by prominent citizens of Quebec to enable him to study in Italy, and there, after a few years, he suddenly became well known for a careful and exact reproduction he made of a painting by Correggio, for which the King of Parma knighted him. Falardeau afterwards settled in Florence and married a niece of the Pope, and so became to the pious Quebec of his day a singular example of what true success in the arts could mean. Antoine Plamondon and Théophile Hamel were other young men who went in for doing such work, but they stopped short of making a career out of it as Falardeau had done. Portraiture was more their ideal.

By the middle of the nineteenth century, as Jean-Paul Lemieux has said concerning the arts in Quebec : " To have one's portrait done became the rage of the town. . . . Everyone who was somebody had his features fixed on canvas for posterity. Both Plamondon and Hamel left a great number of these portraits. In fact there is at least one in every old Quebec family. The stiff conventional pose, elaborate coiffure and complicated dress of the ladies, and the dignified look of the gentlemen reflect but too well the stuffy Victorian interiors."

Neither Plamondon nor Hamel ever attempted landscape painting, although in the charming *La Chasse aux Tourtes* (Plate 4) Plamondon has used landscape as a background to his portraits of three boys.

The first artist to awaken Canadians to the beauty of the countryside, the hills and the forest in their autumn and winter garb, was Cornelius Krieghoff. He was a man whose early life was cloaked in vague exploits, including those typical of a wandering soldier of fortune, for he came from Germany and joined the American Army and fought in the Seminole Indian wars in Florida. But, previous to that, his early training had been as an art student in Dusseldorf, Germany. So, when he fell in love with a French-Canadian girl, whom he had met in Vermont, and deserted from the army in order to marry her and come to Canada, we find him taking up the practice of painting again in order to earn his living and support his family. He dwelt first at Longueuil, across the St. Lawrence River from Montreal, and later in Quebec City, where his work became well known.

He was a gay dog and a wine-bibber, a frequenter of taverns. Yet he managed to wander far enough afield from the city streets to recognise the charm of autumn foliage on northern rivers, and of winter snows on Laurentian hillsides. He emphasised the rich red colouring of sunsets and he was able to give a sharp and glistening brilliance to his renderings of ice and snow. His canvases were widely sold, both in Quebec and in England—so widely, indeed, that as he grew older he succumbed to the ignoble temptation of sitting in his studio and slyly making copy after copy of his own popular works to meet the demand.

The first artists of English birth or descent to appear in this country were various travellers, mainly army officers and engineers, who before the days of photography were accustomed to keep a record of their trips in sketches and water-colours. In what were then the colonies of New Brunswick and Nova Scotia there were also to be found early in the nineteenth century a few amateur artists who painted, for their own amusement, the outdoor scenes of their pioneer environment. One such picture is of Fredericton, New Brunswick (Plate 3); it was done in 1823 by some local artist whose name has been lost to us.

In the newer settlements of Upper Canada—in what is now Ontario—the first native painter of any consequence was Paul Kane. He was brought up in the town of York, now Toronto, and after some desultory art studies abroad he returned to Canada in 1844. Two years afterwards, fired with tales of the fur trade and the Indians, he set out to visit the great lone land of the western plains. Reading his book, *The Wanderings of an Artist among the Indians of North America*, one sees how closely he was able to link art with adventure. He did many paintings afterwards from the sketches

18

he had made during his travels. What interests us largely in them to-day is their reportorial exactitude, their detailed and precise depictions of the games and occupations, the clothing and weapons and the badges of office, in fact, of all the anthropological data he thought worth while to collect about the Indian tribes and chiefs he visited during his journeys.

After Confederation, the arts in Canada went through a short period of awkward adolescence. Very stuffily and in colonial fashion, the institutions of Victorian England now began to be imitated. Drawing masters established themselves in many towns, the first small art academies opened their doors, and various art societies were formed, including the Royal Canadian Academy, which obtained its charter in 1882. A more accurate sign, however, of the attitude of that period towards the arts was the state of the National Gallery which, after being founded in 1880 by the then Governor-General of Canada, the Marquis of Lorne, was left to languish ; thus, for many years, it had to hang its few pictures on the walls of several small rooms adjoining a permanent exhibition of stuffed fish in the Fisheries Building in Ottawa.

For a long time, strong prejudices existed against the presentation of the nude in sculpture and painting. These were severe enough, as is revealed in these lines from Samuel Butler's well-known satirical poem about Montreal, which describes how, during a visit he made to that city in 1875, he found casts of Grecian statuary hidden away for prudery's sake in a museum store-room :

> " Stowed away in a Montreal lumber room
> The Discobolus standeth and turneth his face to the wall ;
> Dusty, cobweb-covered, maimed and set at naught,
> Beauty lieth in an attic and no man regardeth :
> O God ! O Montreal ! "

But a few years later these prejudices had moderated to such an extent that an uninspired but technically facile young artist, Paul Peel, was able to build up a comfortable living for himself in Europe by producing senti-mental nude or semi-nude studies for sale to the richer folk back home in Canada. New tastes like this were often shoddy and second-hand, based not on any real sense of appreciation, but rather upon a falsely sophisticated imitation of current modes abroad. Those artists who remained at home and devoted themselves to more indigenous subjects stood little chance of obtaining success. Here and there, however, a few managed to persevere until they reached eventual prominence. One such was Homer Watson, who, largely self-trained, kept his eyes close to the subjects he knew best, the lush farm-lands of the Grand Valley in Western Ontario, which he painted with a sincere, if hardly prepossessing, vision. There was also Horatio Walker, who transposed to Canadian farm scenes the Barbizon style for pastoral land-scapes. His talent was considerable and he was soon able to sell to wealthy collectors in New York and Chicago and Montreal dozens of canvases every year of cows and oxen or of other scenes of habitant life on the Island of Orleans where he lived. He had, however, his more original moments of creation, as, for example, *The Royal Mail* (Plate 7).

With a background as static as this, it took years before the more experimental and creative tendencies of nineteenth-century art, as they were then manifest in Europe, could make themselves felt in Canada.

There was, for example, a time lag of about thirty years between the advent of impressionism in France and its arrival in Canada. This analysis of light, this search for colour in shadows, this discovery that snow was not white but a patchwork of mauve and pinks and purples, was finally introduced into Canada at the turn of the century by a young painter, Maurice Cullen, who had studied previously for six years in Paris.

Cullen, who was born in Newfoundland, had been brought to Canada as a child, and upon his return from France he made Montreal his permanent home. In that city he endured bitter struggles in order to gain a meagre livelihood before he at last, after many years, achieved a fairly steady sale of his works. He loved to depict the St. Lawrence in winter, snow blowing in cloudy gusts, Montreal streets with sleighs and blanketed horses. Often he would work outdoors in bitterly cold weather, in order to be able to paint, exactly as he saw it, the light from the winter sun falling on snow or on vapour arising from the partly frozen river. While emphasis on the design of the picture surface was not by any means one of the strong points of the impressionist technique, Cullen could, nevertheless, compose with considerable sureness, as shown in his better work such as *Shipyard, Lauzon, in Winter* (Plate 6). Unfortunately he was not able to find in the Montreal of his generation that meeting of appreciative minds which might have encouraged him to exert to the full the creative powers he undoubtedly possessed. He faltered sometimes, and finally, partly because such work sold more readily, he began more and more to engage in the repetitive production of scenes of snow-covered Laurentian hills and lakes, which compositions, despite their popularity, seem monotonous in contrast to his more subtle paintings of city wharfs and urban streets in winter.

During the period from 1886 to 1921, when fresh currents of influence were developing everywhere in western art, the soundest and most stimulating of Canadian art teachers was William Brymner, who for years was director of art classes at the Art Association of Montreal. Although born in Scotland, his early schooling had been entirely in Canada. Afterwards he studied painting for seven years at the Académie Julian and elsewhere in Paris. Upon his return to Montreal, he strove constantly to maintain an intelligent awareness of all that was new and experimental in modern art ; he was a liberal-minded teacher who allowed his pupils to move forward in those inclinations to which their talents seemed best to fit them. Those he knew

II. A. Y. JACKSON (1882-   )
"Red Maple"
Oil: $31\frac{1}{4}'' \times 38\frac{1}{4}''$. *National Gallery of Canada, Ottawa*

as young friends, or encouraged as students, ranged across a whole epoch of Canadian art from James Wilson Morrice to Prudence Heward. While his own work usually lacked any particular impress of personality, he yet often painted landscapes of solid conviction, and in his old age he freed himself enough from the impositions of learning to be able to obtain an extraordinary intimacy of feeling in domestic scenes like this charming *Woman Sewing* (Plate 5).

During their creative years, Brymner, who was active until his death in 1935, and Cullen, who lived until 1934, were able to observe the growth and ultimate coming-of-age of Canadian art.

As it approached maturity, Canadian painting now entered upon two separate but equally significant paths of development. One tendency was personal in origin, individual and delicate to a degree, expatriate almost in conclusion and international in reference ; the other was a group movement, firmly regionalist in philosophy, and more bold than sensitive in expression. The first of these great achievements was centred in one man, James Wilson Morrice, who although he lived a fair part of his life abroad, can yet be regarded as perhaps the greatest painter Canada has produced. The second, more co-operative in realisation, was related to the avowed nationalism of a number of artists who lived and worked in Toronto. This movement culminated in 1920 in the founding of the Group of Seven.

These developments are outlined at length in some of the essays which follow. But first, the careers of three painters of talent who were on the fringe of such achievements, although they never quite took part in them to the full, should be noted.

In 1890 Marc-Aurele de Foy Suzor-Coté went from the country town of Arthabaska in Quebec to study in France, and in the same year Morrice left Montreal for Paris. We have no record that the two men met although France retained them both for many years. But, unlike Morrice, this young French Canadian only ventured a step or two into the realms of the modern spirit in art. After spending seventeen years abroad, he returned to Canada in 1907. Back in his home town, he concentrated upon depicting the traditional subjects of the neighbourhood. He enjoyed painting the sturdy peasants from the surrounding farms, particularly when he found them at home, relaxed and smoking their pipes before the stove or comfortably dozing in good old-fashioned Quebec rocking-chairs. Such figures excited his imagination greatly and he also did small sculptures of them in clay and metal. Unfortunately he never could quite bridge the gap between his genuine desire to interpret the life of rural Quebec and his equally strong yearnings to emulate the factitious glories of the Salon des Beaux-Arts in Paris. As he grew older, he indulged these latter fancies more and more by producing large oils of nudes displayed in monumental poses.

Clarence Gagnon, a native son of Montreal, took to painting the Quebec village as a picturesque fragment of the Canadian scene. He, too, like Morrice and Suzor-Coté, spent a good portion of his life in Paris, where he first obtained a reputation for his etchings of Venice, and later, of Normandy and Brittany. For a while he seems to have come directly under the influence of Morrice, especially when he painted beach scenes in Brittany, but these, despite obvious similarities in composition, never did obtain that elusive quality of timelessness which the best works of Morrice always have. After 1909, Gagnon came back to live for some few years in Canada. As a subject to paint, Baie St. Paul, nestling amidst the steep and wooded hillsides of Charlevoix County on the north shore of the St. Lawrence River, attracted him most. He afterwards returned to Paris, where he continued to paint canvases based on his earlier sketches of Quebec villages. Also, by going on occasional winter visits to Norway, he managed to refresh his memories of northern atmosphere and the colouring of snow. Later he obtained commissions from French publishers to illustrate *de luxe* editions of books on Canadian themes ; he received great praise in particular for a series of monotypes he prepared for reproduction in the book, *Maria Chapdelaine.* His style, however, while it developed in technical applications, never did progress much further in æsthetic understanding during those last years of his career. His best work is undoubtedly to be found in those first satisfactory renderings he did earlier of Baie St. Paul and its nearby villages and farmsteads. One such canvas of a village street is reproduced as Plate 12.

The link between that romantic feeling, which Suzor-Coté and Gagnon had for Quebec landscape, and the more decorative but yet basically naturalistic approach, which A. Y. Jackson has emphasised in recent years, can be traced in the work of A. H. Robinson. This artist, after studying in Paris, had returned to teach in his home town of Hamilton, Ontario. Then about 1908 he took to doing outdoor sketches of Quebec landscape, and after moving to Montreal in 1909 he concentrated almost entirely on such subjects. Snowbound villages in winter, the St. Lawrence with its floating ice in the spring, and in summer the green and quiet valleys and wooded hills of the Eastern Townships of Quebec, were the unchanging objects of his affection. What is remarkable, however, is that no matter how much he became enamoured of such scenes, he rarely weakened his perception by going out of his way to underline their romantic aspects as Gagnon too often had done. Many of his small oil sketches possess that instantaneous recording of visual stimulus which makes them as pleasant, in their own unpretentious way, as are any of the somewhat similar compositions done at that time by A. Y. Jackson. The gaily-coloured sleighs drawn by plodding and often blanketed horses, which Krieghoff first depicted, Robinson now also took as the motif for many of his sketches. These he employed as the subject of his best-known canvas, *Returning from Easter Mass*, which is in the Art Gallery of Toronto.

Despite their personal differences of outlook, Cullen and Suzor-Coté, Gagnon and Robinson, and to a lesser extent Morrice and Jackson, were all closely dependent upon the traditional elements of the Quebec landscape for their visual stimulus.

Here we must emphasise, lest its importance be forgotten later, that the cultivated countryside of Quebec, recalling as it does human toil and struggle and the slow domination of man over nature, has provided as fundamental an influence on landscape painting in Canada as have any of those cruder and more untouched aspects of wild nature which came, in the second decade of the twentieth century, to symbolise Canadian nationalism in art.

JAMES WILSON MORRICE (1865-1924)

Into the Stream of Modern Art

THE story of James Wilson Morrice, expatriate son of a wealthy Montreal family, is that of a wanderer between continents, of a painter in advance of his time in Canada, who spent much of his life in the more receptive atmosphere of Paris but who yet returned home year after year to sketch the winter landscape of his native province of Quebec. In Europe he frequented some of the most cosmopolitan society of the day, and numbered amongst his friends such novelists as Somerset Maugham and Arnold Bennett, both of whom knew him well and have recorded their memories of him in several of their books. There is, for instance, a distinct resemblance between him and the character Priam Farll in Bennett's *Buried Alive*.

His personal vision of the world is preserved for us in at least five hundred small panels, about two hundred canvases, and a few rare but highly prized water-colours, which are to be found to-day in public and private collections on three continents. A horse and sleigh crossing the St. Lawrence in winter, dark-shawled Italian women in the public gardens of Venice, an Arab with a donkey on the beach at Tangiers, a group of French artisans on a Sunday outing along the banks of the Seine, such are the subjects. Diverse enough, yet somehow alike, for over each hangs an atmosphere—to describe a visual sensation only too inadequately in words—of dreamlike and languid meditation.

Born in Montreal in 1865, the son of a prominent merchant of Scottish extraction, Morrice was, as he grew up, destined by his parents to enter the legal profession. After graduating from the University of Toronto and from Osgoode Hall, he quickly deserted the law for painting. Already he had done many water-colours, but his first real apprenticeship in art began after he was twenty-five, when he went to Paris.

He worked independently and with little reference to schools or teachers. His painting went through many variations in style, and he did some experiments, first in the manner of Whistler and much later of Matisse. Yet there was always something in every one of his paintings which was very much his own. French critics have said, for example, that by setting his figures, like solid immovable counters in the landscape, he was able to induce a feeling of gentle melancholy, and that his psychological overtones were not Gallic but vaguely Anglo-Saxon. Equally original, they said, was " the rose of an exquisite delicacy," which he employed as an almost imperceptible background in most of his paintings. If you study the canvases of Morrice

24

you will notice that this rose creeps into his pigments almost from the beginning. He discovered this colouring in some of his first attempts to depict Quebec scenery in winter, back in the nineties, and he seemed never to forget it. That touch of ruddiness in the atmosphere is something peculiar to the Canadian skies in winter. European visitors often remark that one of the most vivid impressions they have of Canada is of this diffused and pinkish light so noticeable at times in our snow-bound skies. They do not see it in the greyer atmosphere of northern or central Europe, or on the clearer horizons of the Mediterranean.

The feeling which Morrice had for Canadian landscape, particularly its winter atmosphere, was true. But in his Quebec paintings he was not trying to tell one, as in a lesson, that this was nationalist landscape and northern air and skies ; his approach, as can be seen from this canvas, *Ice Bridge over the St. Lawrence* (Plate I), was a much more subtle and more subjective one than that.

The Group of Seven came after him, and A. Y. Jackson, who, as a student, had always been strongly moved by Morrice's works, was, in a sense, one of his disciples. But Morrice did not have that same urgency of belief in Canadian nature which Jackson and his colleagues did. Every artist finds his stimulus in his own way, and Morrice, it is safe to assert, found his mainly by travelling. Also, as he grew older, he mingled in Paris with those advanced painters who had formed the Salon d'Automne, and this brought him close in understanding to men like Matisse, who tried to organise the design of the picture surface by modulations, changes and contrasts in colour, as much as by line and perspective.

His paintings were eagerly acquired during his lifetime by discriminating collectors in Paris. Appreciation of him by his fellow-artists also grew with the years. After his death, Matisse addressed to the editor of *L'Art et Les Artistes* a sincere letter in tribute to his friend, whom he called " the artist with the delicate eye, so pleasing with a touching tenderness in the rendering of landscapes of closely allied values ; " at the same time, Dunoyer de Segonzac organised a memorial exhibition of his work at the Salon d'Automne, an honour which that distinguished organisation had rarely bestowed before on a foreign artist.

Similar recognition, especially for his later paintings, was to arrive more slowly in Canada. Those earlier and more sombre snow-scenes, done with pigment laid on thickly and with considerable over-painting, such as *Winter, Ste. Anne de Beaupré* (Plate 9), had sold well in Montreal, but after 1908, when more subtle and less obviously naturalistic colours began to creep into his painting and his style became more broadly calligraphic, his work found few buyers at home. In disgust, he ceased to exhibit in Montreal and soon forsook Canada entirely, except for one or two brief visits in 1917 and 1919 when he was *en route* from Paris to the West Indies.

The most spontaneous of his creations were those done about 1919 following a winter spent in Trinidad. In those last canvases of his, of which this one, *Landscape, Trinidad* (Plate 10), is an excellent example, it appeared as if he had decided, once the values of his colours were true, to leave his drawing as spontaneous, as simple and as personal as possible. But he did not have many years left in which to paint with this new freedom, for he died in 1924 in Tunis while on one of his solitary voyages.

The creations of his prime—those canvases of lush foliage, of tropical waters and sandy coves—were not exhibited in Canada until many years afterwards. During the early nineteen-thirties, however, when they first began to be shown in Montreal, they helped by their stimulus and example to encourage various of our younger Canadian painters to move forward into the paths of a broader and more unfettered art.

III. J. E. H. MacDONALD, R.C.A. (1873-1932)
" Autumn in Algoma (Fall of the Leaf) "
Oil: 47½″ × 59½″. *National Gallery of Canada, Ottawa*

A. Y. JACKSON (1882-)

The Growth of Nationalism

BETWEEN Winnipeg in the west and the farmlands of southern Ontario in the east, there stretches for 1500 miles a vast and monotonous rocky plateau. Its hollows are filled with innumerable small lakes and ponds, while the rest of its surface is covered with stunted birch and pine. Here and there, its low rolling horizon is broken by a few sombre, forbidding escarpments of exposed rock. Known geologically as the Pre-Cambrian Shield, it is for the most part a great wilderness, unsettled except for a few mining towns and scattered villages built round pulp and paper mills and railway roundhouses. An ocean, as it were, separating the Canadian west from the Canadian east, it forms a geographical barrier which complicates, at the same time as it restricts, the life, the culture and the economics of the Dominion.

The first artists to be attracted to this northern land of turbulent waters and silent lakes were those few hardy lovers of the outdoors who liked to combine sketching expeditions with canoeing trips along its distant streams, one of which they called " the forty miles of white water," and others by their Indian names such as Mississauga and Audinadong. The paintings they made upon their return from these journeys were at first not appreciated, but gradually their forthright renderings of the cruder aspects of Canadian nature began to be accepted by an ever-widening circle of followers. Soon a regionalist school of painters had developed, in whose work the burnt-over forests, the rock-girt lakes and the sharply edged clouds of the northland emerged as the symbols of a purely Canadian movement in landscape art. The four principal figures in this movement were Tom Thomson, A. Y. Jackson, J. E. H. MacDonald and Lawren Harris.

Each of these men had, already by 1914, begun to rebel against that derivative type of painting related to the pearly colouring of Dutch landscapes and to the subdued naturalism of the Barbizon School, which was then dominant in Canadian salons.

For the most part, the changes which took place in their painting were brought about by the visual impact of the northern scenery they set out to describe. With A. Y. Jackson, however, there was in the beginning a combination of both learning from abroad and of a new inspiration from Canadian scenes.

Jackson had been born in Montreal and educated there ; then, having already done some work in art, he went in 1910 to Paris to continue his studies. There he was taught much about the use of pure colour in painting and about the scientific approach of the impressionist masters to the analysis of light and shade. On his return to Canada, he first applied this technique in a series of canvases of farm and woodland scenes which he did in the Eastern Townships of Quebec. He soon found, however, that the clear atmosphere of his native Canada called for a more sharply defined treatment than that which he had learned to employ when painting the softer and more mellow landscapes of France.

There were others who agreed with him. Lawren Harris, having seen and liked one of Jackson's paintings in an exhibition, wrote to tell him of the interest some of the younger artists in Ontario were taking in sketching the north woods. So Jackson came to Toronto to meet Harris and the others. He made his first trip to Georgian Bay in 1913, and in 1914 he proceeded north again to Algonquin Park, this time with Tom Thomson.

Jackson has recently put down his recollections of those years when the vision of a new nationalism in Canadian art was beckoning him on by canoe and portage from one pine and sumac fringed lake to another.

"The country was exciting," he recalls, "the atmosphere clear and sharp, the colours bright—crude, if you will. The villages scattered, some of them just shack towns, the landscape untidy and ragged as you went north, swampy, rocky, wolf-ridden, a land burnt or scuttled and flooded by lumber companies, with rivers and numerous lakes all over it, and on top of all this variety there were changes of season such as they hardly knew in Europe. In autumn it flamed with red and gold, in winter wrapped in a blanket of dazzling snow, and in springtime it roared with running waters and surged with new life. So why stick to the barnyard, why paint cows and sheep and rural tranquillity?"

In 1920 the Group of Seven was formed, and Jackson soon became its principal spokesman. "We frankly abandoned our attempts at literal painting," he wrote, "and treated our subjects with the freedom of a decorative designer."

Year in and year out, Jackson sought as earnestly to paint the snows of Canada as he did its forests and lakes and mountains. In early spring, when the melting snow lay heaped in ridges on the fields, he would visit the old settled parishes of the lower St. Lawrence region, and there, tramping through the countryside on snowshoes, with sketch-box in hand, he became known to the local inhabitants as "Père Raquette," that is, "Father Snowshoes." In his best canvases of these scenes the snow is revealed, not as something pretty, like icing on a cake, but rather for what it is, most of the time, a rough and corrugated and wind-blown covering to the landscape.

He was the first Canadian artist to be honoured by a motion picture describing his work. This film, prepared by the National Gallery of Canada and the National Film Board of Canada, was done in colour and has been shown widely both in Canada and abroad. Entitled *Canadian Landscape*, it demonstrates how Jackson first makes small sketches on wooden panels out of doors, and how he later works them up in his studio into larger compositions on canvas.

Although he continues to paint in Quebec each spring, the broad, unending horizons of the western plains have begun to attract him more and more. Teaching now in the summer at the Banff School of Fine Arts, he frequently goes on sketching tours into the foothills of southern Alberta or farther north along the Alaska Highway.

One need only look at a selection of his sketches to note how remarkable is the sensitivity with which he records such changes of climate and atmosphere. For instance, take his sketches of southern Alberta. A month previously he may have been in the Quebec countryside where, in the moist spring air, he would have been depicting, with what for him are rare touches of sensuous gaiety, those colourful scenes of melting snow and horses and red sleds on drifted roads. But now in the west he starts in at once putting down, with sure strokes of colour and with what is visible realism, even from the moment of his first arrival there, the dry brittle sense of distance in the prairie landscape or the deep cast of shadows marked by a harsh sun on a semi-arid range of hills.

Each year, during the late autumn and winter, when he lives in his studio in Toronto, he takes the most interesting of his sketches and, using them as motifs, produces from them a number of large canvases. Sometimes in his studio compositions the decorative emphasis is so dominating that his usual more subtle references to local atmosphere are overwhelmed ; yet, in his best canvases, he usually manages to preserve, without any noticeable loss of impact in the transition, the geographical validity of his original sketches.

In recent years his compositions have been much in demand, and the economic security he has obtained from the ready sale of his paintings has enabled him to become a traveller, a seeker of new scenes, more especially of those on the pioneer or wilderness fringe of Canada, the fur-trading posts of Baffin Island, the mines of the Northwest Territories, the airfields of the Yukon and the upland grazing lands of the Cariboo district of British Columbia.

An English observer, Wyndham Lewis, has said aptly enough that Jackson's sketching trips are rigorous campaigns in which it is " nature-the-enemy " whom he seeks to conquer. Certainly when he travels to the far north and the west, he is no mere lover of the outdoors seeking pleasure in his cult ; he is rather the tireless explorer. On his expeditions he does not let the simple rigours of weather defeat him ; he regrets a morning or an afternoon when he cannot make some kind of sketch in the open air. With a puritanical doggedness, he is willing to face the ugly as well as the beautiful in nature, and he brings back both the grim and the pleasant.

TOM THOMSON (1877-1917)

A Man in a Canoe

AS a painter, Tom Thomson gave us his own "private, splendid vision of the north country," and, in his bold sketches of forest and river, he expressed, as one of his admirers so aptly put it, " the emotions which make a man a woodsman." Yet he was not, as some would have us naïvely believe, a mere untutored and simple *voyageur* who suddenly became, through the impact of the scenery he loved, a primitive artist of signal power. The truth is much less romantic than the legend, but dramatic enough in its own way.

From 1901 to 1914 Thomson had not been living " passionately with the wild ; " he was in fact a commercial artist, earning his living by designing covers for leaflets and title pages for catalogues, or by doing other more routine jobs in printing and engraving plants. Born and educated in rural Ontario, he had wandered west to the Pacific Coast as a young man and had become an apprentice in an engraving firm in Seattle, Washington ; afterwards he had returned to Canada and obtained similar employment in Toronto. Although he had been brought up on a farm near the shores of Georgian Bay and had gone fishing and tramping in the woods as a boy, he had had little real experience of " roughing it in the bush " until in 1912 he had taken a long canoe trip into one of the remoter areas of northern Ontario. But he seemed to have had a natural love for the outdoor life, and he soon was able to paddle a canoe in a stiff breeze and follow a trail in the bush along with the best of the guides and the trappers. The interest he now took in painting was related directly to the growth of his devotion to forest ways. His originality as a landscape artist and his skill as a woodsman developed hand in hand, one as it were deriving sustenance from the other.

All his early training as a commercial designer had been of a journeyman nature. By way of a hobby he had, however, done a few water-colours ; then in 1911 he joined the firm of Grip Limited, in Toronto, where he met J. E. H. MacDonald and Arthur Lismer, who persuaded him to try his hand at sketching in oils.

From the canoeing expedition in 1912 he brought back a number of small oil sketches on wooden panels. These were sombre studies of pine islands and dark water and rough and rocky shore lines ; while somewhat meticulous in execution, they yet gave evidence of a true sympathy for the grim northland. His friends now encouraged him to do large compositions as well and to concentrate on painting as a profession. The idea of making art his life's work did not at first appeal to him, but finally he decided to try it, and by

IV.   TOM THOMSON (1877-1917)
" Tea Lake Dam "

Oil sketch on wooden panel: $8\frac{1}{2}'' \times 10\frac{1}{2}''$.   *National Gallery of Canada, Ottawa*

1914 he had deserted his job to spend the autumn and early winter painting in the north.

" During his brief career as a painter," as his friend Arthur Lismer has written, " he passed from the ordinary amateurish methods of the beginner to the stature of a mature artist with a powerful technique of brushwork, design and use of colour—sensitive, vibrant and spatial. All of which happened in the space of five or six years from his early start as a painter in 1911 to the time of his death."

His death was sudden and mysterious. In 1917 he came north in the early spring to his cabin in Algonquin Park, where he spent many weeks recording each changing aspect of the spring landscape, from early woodland flowers and rushing streams to the first buds of foliage on the birch trees. One morning he met one of his friends, a forest ranger, and told him that he had finished this series of sketches. Soon afterwards he was found drowned, not far from his overturned canoe, on a July day of that year.

Few of his larger oil paintings, of which he only completed some thirty or so during his brief career, were sold while he was alive. But one patron, Dr. James McCallum, an eye specialist in Toronto, had as early as 1913 understood the extent of his talents and had bought enough of his sketches to give him, for a while at least, some sense of temporary security. Also the National Gallery of Canada recognised his talents during his lifetime by purchasing three of his canvases, including the important *Spring Ice* and *Northern River* (Plate 17). Yet the sale of a few sketches and canvases was not enough in itself to support him, and for many months on end from 1915 to 1917 he had to eke out his living by acting as a guide in Algonquin Park.

Not entirely self-taught, he was able to borrow at first some *art nouveau* arrangements from his training in commercial design. He also picked up a knowledge of impressionist colour harmonies through association with A. Y. Jackson, with whom he shared a studio in Toronto in 1914. But, in practice, when it came to the essentials of what he wanted to paint—the log-run on a stream roaring with the flood of April rains or the " single tree against the evening sky of the north "—he found that he really had no European idiom or point of reference to fall back upon. To present the Canadian northland, as he felt it and saw it, he began to depend more and more on his own awakening vision, on his own solitary moods of reflection and thought, " seeking seclusion," as Lismer has said, and " finding companionship in the friendliness of things like skylines and weather."

While he was shy and as happy when alone as with friends, he was, however, not aloof ; for instance, he often took other artists along on his canoeing and sketching trips. Jackson, recalling his first meeting with him in 1913, states : " You liked Thomson right away, a quiet friendly chap, something of the Indian in his bearing, a kind of indolence that changed to sudden alertness and quick movement when occasion arose." And later, of

31

those days in Algonquin Park : " Thomson liked doing all the paddling while I sat in the bottom of the canoe, keeping a look-out for subjects to sketch. He paddled like an Indian, using the weight of his body more than his arms, and he could keep going all day with no sign of fatigue. . . . To the few natives, Thomson's name was like a password."

One remembers in this connection the tribute which Ray Atherton, a former United States Ambassador to Canada, paid to him in a speech delivered in his honour in 1947, thirty years after his death.

" He was a man in a canoe," said Atherton, " who succeeded in explaining to us something of the secret of the countless men in canoes, something of the story they never told through the long centuries that they moved silently up and down the waterways of our continent. . . . The men in canoes, the men alone but not lonely, the Indians first and then the French and those who came later, these are the men who slowly, over the centuries, built Canada. They had something more in their hearts than money from furs. One of these men, named Thomson, has been able to tell us what they had in their hearts."

Those who see this passionate relationship between Thomson and the northern forests and rivers sense it particularly in his best sketches done between 1915 and 1917, such as this one of a logging dam on a river, reproduced as Plate IV. These sketches and most of his later canvases, also, are exact and yet daring in their bold realism of execution ; to all those who have travelled these same streams, avoided these same swamps and muskegs, or who have ventured into these same hidden lakes lined with pine and underbrush, his sketches provide vivid and nostalgic memories of adventuresome days.

9. JAMES WILSON MORRICE, R.C.A. (1865-1924)
" Winter, Ste. Anne de Beaupré "
Oil: 23½″ × 31½″.   *Louis W. Coldwell, Esq., Montreal*

10. JAMES WILSON MORRICE, R.C.A. (1865-1924)
"Landscape, Trinidad"
Oil: 26″ × 32″. National Gallery of Canada, Ottawa

11. JAMES WILSON MORRICE, R.C.A. (1865-1924)
" Algiers "
Water-colour: 9″ × 11½″.   Hart House, University of Toronto

12. CLARENCE A. GAGNON, R.C.A. (1881-1942)
" Street, Village in the Laurentians "
Oil: 21½″ × 28½″. R. S. McLaughlin, Esq., Oshawa, Ontario

13.   ALBERT H. ROBINSON, R.C.A. (1881-   )
"Brome Lake"
Oil: 11″ × 12¾″.   *Dominion Gallery, Montreal*

14. A. Y. JACKSON (1882-   )
" Georgian Bay, November "
Oil: 21″ × 26″.   Hart House, University of Toronto

15. A. Y. JACKSON (1882-   )
" Sun Gleams, near Bic "
Oil: 21⅜″ × 26⅛″.   *W. R. Watson, Esq., Montreal*

16. A. Y. JACKSON (1882-   )
" The North Shore, Baffin Island "
Oil: 21″ × 26″. East York Collegiate Institute, Toronto

J. E. H. MacDONALD (1873-1932)

Painter of the Forest

THOSE who worked with J. E. H. MacDonald, before 1912, when he was for a few years the art director of a commercial engraving plant in Toronto, describe him as " this tall, thin designer, with his halo of red hair, his love of Henry Thoreau, Walt Whitman and lyric verse " who " always had a book on hand to take up in any spare time he had ; " they also speak of his " self-contained . . . retiring temperament." But one needed to know him, away from the busy turmoil of city life, if one really wished to understand his essential character. His happiest days were spent when he was able to leave the city for his home in Thornhill, a small village near Toronto, where in quiet and almost rural surroundings he could plant potatoes, make axe-handles or sketch the apple tree growing beside his kitchen window. There also, when evening came and friends and neighbours had gathered round a bonfire in the garden, he would sit in the dim light and retail many simple and homely anecdotes of the outdoors which he had picked up during his painting excursions into the north woods and the western mountains. When fields and forests or the ways of the common man were being discussed, all his " quiet and reserve " would drop and he would become expansive, gay and even verbose.

He was interested in everything in nature and not only as a painter. " He returned from sketching trips," it has been said, " with much more than sketches ; moose skulls, deer horns, bones, rocks, plants, young trees, tarred rope, shells, stumps gnawed by beaver, horse-shoes, axe-heads and notebooks of observations." On his travels his favourite companions were the two volumes, *The Maine Woods* and *Walden*, by Thoreau. As his son states : " He thought *Walden* contained more ideas for its weight than any other book." Yet the convictions and outlook which guided his own actions were based, perhaps, not so much on the philosophy of others as on his own quiet ponderings amid the silence of forest and mountain, or more simply when, at home, he took his daily walks " up the lane " and across the fields.

His hatred of humbug, his loathing of injustice, his dislike of tradition whether in art or religion, are expressed in the sturdily homespun poems he wrote. These were published after his death under the title, *West by East*. But related more intimately to his painting are those letters, giving his impressions of the landscape, which he sent home from his travels in the northern hills. In them and in a few articles he prepared afterwards for publication, he dwells, in loving and almost romantic detail, upon all those subtle changes of colour which came over the forest in September and early October, when the hills become crimson and scarlet.

Here is his description of a scene he painted during the late autumn in Algoma : " Birch woods, that were dense yellow in the morning, were open grey by night. But the wild cherry leaves still hung as though the high fifes and violins were to finish the great concert of colour. They were another of the notable little graces of the bush, daintily hung in every shade from palest yellow to deep crimson against the big blue-gold hills of the Montreal Valley. The sound of the bush changed with the lessening leaves—no softened rustle all about, but the hollow soughing of a million trees from far heights and valleys. And there was a deeper note from the waterfalls, for the rains had filled the courses again after the drought of summer. There was an exhilaration for the sketchers in working by rapid and fall."

Yes, it was sheer " exhilaration " which led them on, these " sketchers," the three artists, MacDonald, Lawren Harris and F. H. Johnston. They were making that autumn their first discovery of the picturesque scenery of Algoma. This district along the north-eastern shore of Lake Superior was a much wilder, more formidable region than was the territory round Georgian Bay and Algonquin Park, which they had visited in other years. Lawren Harris chose to depict both the loneliness and the awesome sense of distance of this land. As for MacDonald, he went rather to the forest itself and out of its tangled complexity he wove the tapestry of his compositions. During this and other trips to Algoma he painted dozens of small oil sketches on wooden panels, which glow with rich pigment, often strongly and heavily applied. But his masterpieces are the great canvases, such as *October Shower Gleam* (Plate 21) and *Autumn in Algoma* (Plate III), which he did afterwards in his studio.

But MacDonald was never a man to consolidate his talents upon the depiction of one aspect of nature only. His early paintings, before the days of the northland outings, had been of the ravines and farmlands in the countryside near Toronto ; these were subjects which he did not even now entirely forsake. For example, *Cattle by the Creek* (Plate 20) was finished in the same year as he made his first eventful trip to Algoma. In its own placid way, it is as thoroughly Canadian an achievement as are any of those more powerful Algoma canvases.

In an earlier period of his career as a painter, from 1907 to 1911, he had concentrated, on Sundays and holidays, on painting the countryside of southern Ontario, in compositions which, while native and original, yet showed the hard struggle he had put into the making of them. Those early efforts, with their emphasis on visual realism, had given him a solid grounding in design and draughtsmanship. He later acquired a more personal mastery of colour, as the result of painstaking experiments he made in adapting the

V. ARTHUR LISMER, R.C.A. (1885-   )
" Rain in the North Country "
Oil: 32″ × 40″. National Gallery of Canada, Ottawa

colour harmonies of the impressionists to his own needs. From one such early experiment came the well-known picture, *Tracks and Traffic*, now in the Art Gallery of Toronto.

As he became more sure of himself, a new sense of pleasure entered to enliven his passages of drawing and brushwork. This is already evident in *Cattle by the Creek*, and it becomes even more noticeable in his Algoma sketches. A truly unrestrained delight in the gaiety of pigment is reached in the canvas, *Leaves in the Brook* (1922), now in a private collection, where the whole composition centres upon a blazing riot of autumn leaves which have fallen upon the rocks and waters of a swift-flowing stream.

The chronicle of his life is simple and can be recorded briefly. An English boy, who had been brought up in the cathedral city of Durham, he had come to Canada with his parents when he was fourteen and had received his art education in Hamilton, Ontario. What he learned at art school there probably neither harmed nor helped him much. Later he was apprenticed to an engraving firm in Toronto and afterwards worked for three years in a commercial studio in England ; he then returned to Toronto, where he was for many years employed as a designer by Grip Limited, a company where he had as his fellow-employees many of the artists, such as Lismer and Varley, who afterwards were associated with him in the Group of Seven. There, too, he made friends with Tom Thomson.

From 1912 to 1920 he tried to earn his living mainly from easel painting, but his income from the sale of canvases proved to be pitifully meagre, and in 1921 he was glad enough to accept a teaching position offered him at the Ontario College of Art. He subsequently became principal of that institution. On his holidays in the last years of his life, he went mainly to the Rocky Mountains. Their distant solitudes seemed to satisfy that continual hunger which he possessed for meditation amidst the unspoiled scenes of nature. He now changed his style, but his experiments in simplification of pattern were not always successful. Many of these larger alpine canvases, as well as some paintings he did in Nova Scotia of beach and ocean, are as flat as any poster. On the other hand, some of the smaller sketches which he did in the Rockies retained his former freedom.

Exhausted by his teaching tasks, he had a severe physical collapse in 1932, and he died in November of that year.

His best paintings are among the masterpieces of Canadian art. They are unaffected and sure, full of a personal sincerity, needing no recourse to regional content or geographical symbolism for their justification. Yet, compared to Jackson and Harris, MacDonald was far from prolific as a painter. Except for a few years, when he sought vainly to exist by the sale of his canvases, he painted mainly to satisfy himself, " to show his pleasure in the landscape," or to present what he himself called in one of his poems, " the common blessing of the air."

ARTHUR LISMER (1885-   )

Teaching as a Significant Career

"WE have a background of epic grandeur," declared Arthur Lismer, "and the modern movement here, which is a return to nature for sustenance, truly expresses all the vigour and strength that is our heritage."

These qualities of "epic grandeur" can be seen clearly enough in some of his own paintings, especially in those like *October on the North Shore* (Plate 23), which he did during the nineteen-twenties following sketching trips he had made to the region of Lake Superior. Out of a range of rocky hills he has created, in this picture, a composition of large and broad dimensions, in which the rough and ready majesty of the Algoma landscape is underlined by means of strong rhythms of line and austere colouring ; also, to give added emphasis to the magnitude of the scene, he has painted a row of starkly outlined clouds rising like distant ramparts in the upper sky.

Yet he had too strong a feeling for gaiety of colour ever to be completely at home in the designing of canvases as massive in construction and as sober in intent as this one is. He did several other pictures of similar nature, but one feels they were more the result of a self-imposed discipline than of any personal inclination ; for instance, even when composing his most sombre paintings, he seemed unable to refrain from adding, here and there, the most unexpected and almost startling passages of lively colour. This tendency towards a certain roguishness in the handling of pigment has, in fact, always been one of the principal characteristics of his work.

Lismer had already had considerable training as an artist before he first set foot in Canada in January, 1911. Born in Yorkshire, he had attended art school in Sheffield and had then gone to the Académie Royale des Beaux-Arts in Antwerp. In London he had seen the famous exhibition of post-impressionist art arranged in 1910 by Roger Fry and had been impressed by the broader use of colour employed by artists like Gauguin and Van Gogh. His early work in Canada, however, was fairly restrained and based almost completely, in a derivative sense, on the broken tonal harmonies of the impressionists ; but, by 1918, as his *" Olympic " with Returned Soldiers* (Plate 24) demonstrates, his use of colour had become more frank and direct. There followed those years when, especially after his first visit, with Lawren Harris, in 1923, to the North Shore of Lake Superior he tried to build up compositions of northern landscape in great patterned blocks of hills and rocks and tree-trunks and burnt stumps. These experiments of his in the decorative treatment of Canadian landscape became more satisfactory in proportion as he

36

was able to relate his interest in colour more directly to them. This can be seen from the reproduction, *Rain in the North Country* (Plate V).

While so many Canadian painters have only taken grudgingly to teaching as a necessary means of livelihood, to Lismer teaching has always appeared to be a significant career in itself. Labouring constantly in this field since 1915, he has made many signal contributions to the improvement of art education in Canada. An exponent of freedom of personality and of creative experiment in art, he continually finds new ways of taking his message to the public. He went on a speaking tour of Canada once ; in his lectures he urged his audiences to relax the vigour of their prejudices : " Approach," he said, " a little to the simplicity of the children," and then, he added, " you will understand what is meant by ' art is a form of expression.' "

After having been in succession Principal of the Halifax School of Art and Vice-Principal of the Ontario College of Art, Lismer moved to the position of Educational Supervisor of the Art Gallery of Toronto in 1927. Under the auspices of that gallery, he then proceeded to build up the Children's Art Centre, which soon became well known throughout the continent. It was based on the idea not of giving children a technical training in perspective and colour values, but rather of releasing in them a sense of joyous adventure, of letting them find, largely by themselves, the means of communicating their ideas, their problems, their aspirations and enthusiasms into confident expression in painting and drawing.

This conception was developed from the pioneering work which Franz Cizek had done earlier among children in Vienna. " There is so much of autumn and winter, but spring comes only once in a lifetime," is a phrase of Cizek's which Lismer often repeats.

In 1936 Lismer spent a year in the Union of South Africa organising children's art classes throughout that country on the invitation of its Government. He also visited and gave lectures in Australia and New Zealand. During 1938-39, when he was Professor of Fine Arts at Teachers College, Columbia University, New York, he was able to take his philosophy directly into the highest academic circles. Since 1940 he has been Educational Supervisor for the Montreal Museum of Fine Arts and has started a Children's Art Centre there ; he is also Assistant Professor of Fine Arts at McGill University.

He sees the day when " creative child art " will be adopted everywhere in formal schooling in Canada, and his methods have already begun to be incorporated into the official educational systems of several of the Canadian provinces. Commenting on this, he wrote recently : " As a social, psychological and artistic effort, encouraged by private organisations and in individual studios, child art only achieves a sparse fulfilment of its purpose. To fit the individual into society is definitely a duty of educational authority in a democracy. Child art will lose something of value when it is moved

37

over into the more official fields of education, but nevertheless its presence there will temper our over-emphasis on the factual and intellectual aspects of education, by infusing the whole field of formal teaching with a new understanding of creativeness in action. . . ." This stands as his hope and outlook for the future.

Now well into his sixties, he paints more than ever during his summer vacations, and recently, on a trip to Newfoundland, he went back to doing a favourite subject of his, the wharves and warehouses of fishing villages, an interest he first acquired when he lived years ago in Halifax. He likes particularly to paint the gear left piled up or chucked around by the fishermen. "These stone anchors—killicks—these traps and cages and floats, these boats and oars, buckets and ropes, many of them made by hand because the fishermen are poor, have a human quality," he says, "and they seem to have as well the same feeling of weather as pine trees." "They are the real abstract," he adds, "they fall into natural positions. To rearrange them into formal still lifes would be to kill them. I am too fond of the things themselves to want to change them into something else."

He has also during the last few years been returning to those first sketching grounds of the Group of Seven, the islands of Georgian Bay, and there, according to his friend Robert Ayre, he has been painting ". . . open water great seas, the wreckage of storms ; tranquil lakes hidden away for surprise ; and the never-ending tenacious writhing life of the Canadian jungle, thrusting up new growth to cover old scars, yet never quite concealing the bare bones of the struggle."

In many ways, one could wish that Lismer had had more time to concentrate upon his own painting, and was not so constantly tied down to educational duties. As it is, he embarks each summer upon various experiments in colour or in composition, only to drop them in the autumn for teaching ; when another summer comes round, often the threads of inspiration have become tangled, and he lets them go, to move off at some new tangent of development. As a result, his significant achievements in art education tend, among the public at large, to overshadow his accomplishments as a painter.

VI. LAWREN HARRIS (1885-   )
"Bylot Island"
Oil: 42½″ × 50½″.   National Gallery of Canada, Ottawa

LAWREN HARRIS (1885-   )

The Search for the Absolute

THE newspaper caption over an exhibition of paintings by Lawren Harris reads " Annoys Some, Stimulates Others." The wording is brisk but the meaning is clear—for controversy and the quickening pulse of æsthetic discussion have always marked every stage of this artist's career.

Harris once described his more academic critics as those who " mumble old, dead catch-phrases " and " praise far-off things," and, to their expostulations that his paintings were " contrary to sound canons of taste," he replied, " Nothing was ever created anywhere, at any time, save it was in defiance of catch-phrases." Also he wrote that " the irrepressible creates ceaselessly fresh moulds for its future widening." In his own work, it is this kind of change into " new moulds," this experimental moving forward, which so often provokes and puzzles not only the general public but also at times even his own immediate colleagues.

During the years following 1910, when Harris, after travels abroad, had come back to Toronto to live, he deliberately set out to combat that hard core of provincial taste which still pervaded the artistic life of that city. Having a flair for philosophic argument picked up during the years he had spent as an art student in Berlin and elsewhere in Germany, he was soon putting his protestations about life and his theories about art and culture into speech and print as well as into his paintings. One of his friends exclaimed at this time that he had both " a streak of Heine and a streak of Whitman."

As he came from a wealthy family, which had made money in the farm implement business in Canada, he could well afford to give full scope to his convictions. On one side he had a mystical bent, but, on the other hand, he had a most definite sense of practical values as well. For example, in 1914 he financed the erection of the commodious Studio Building on Severn Street in Toronto and here various artists of talent, including some of those who later became leaders of the Group of Seven, were able to find permanent working quarters at low rentals. The building also became a centre where they and others could meet, discuss each other's work and debate with enthusiasm the new " Canadian spirit in art."

While Jackson and MacDonald now found the pine-clad and rocky islands of Georgian Bay suitable subjects " to convey the sense of rough dignity and generosity which the nature of the country suggests," Harris, although stimulated equally by such landscapes, felt that there were other less romantic aspects of the Canadian scene which also needed to be treated by the artist. Returning from several seasons of painting in the north country, he went to the crude rawness of the new working-class suburbs of Toronto, and to the slums of Halifax and to those of the mining towns of Cape Breton in Nova Scotia, to find subjects of more urban and social realism.

The compositions of antique brick or plaster-sided houses he had produced some years before in Toronto had been far from severe ; they were rather, as he said, " the natural expression of a love for homely subjects with their roots firmly fixed in the everyday life of all Canadians." In their smooth-flowing surface textures, in their sometimes gay but never blatant modulations of colour, these earlier works of his were, as far as the handling of pigment went, among the most sensitive he has ever painted. But when he turned away from the charm of these fading and dilapidated structures to underline the new and ugly jerry-built dwellings in a cheap suburb seen across backyards drifted with soot-sprinkled snow, as in this picture, *Shacks* (Plate 27), he became intentionally less pleasant in his use of pigment.

During the nineteen-twenties, the broad and rocky panoramas of the North Shore of Lake Superior became the magnet which drew him most. Here were distant horizons of water and sky, precipitous headlands and, to the north, receding levels of rising hills.

" Harris was tending towards bold simplification . . ." writes Jackson of this period. " He needed more space and he found it on the North Shore."

He now set out to analyse the forms of this landscape ; he picked out what were to him its most significant symbols—burnt trees, pine stumps, stark barren islands and clearly edged clouds—and by emphasising their contours and by using colour in pure, often flat, tones he achieved some of his most distinctive compositions. Depth of atmosphere and all mutations of detail, qualities he felt to be derivative from European painting, were now discarded by him, for he was seeing " things as they are in Canada, with the foreground as distinct as the background."

Although certain critics complained that these canvases " were going to discourage immigration to Canada," there were many others who saw them quite differently, who praised them as worthy of the dignity of the Canadian frontier, of the strong pioneer beginnings of the land, or as one newspaper contributor put it, " of the spirit from which the nation started and as a solace to which it can return and start again." Lawren Harris now was called " a preacher . . . who makes the north the text for the whole nation." Those phrases were written in 1927, the year when the Statute of Westminster was passed giving Canada full sovereign powers ; it was also a year of prosperity, of stock-market booms, of gold-mining expansion, of the building of skyscrapers in the cities, yet there were many who already felt, during this feverish period of economic progress, a need for a re-interpretation and a strengthening of both spiritual and national values.

Only by appreciating this background can one understand the fervour with which many of the young students in Canadian universities seized upon these paintings of his as visual proclamations of the stature and meaning of Canada, " the true North, strong and free," and proudly bought reproductions of them to pin upon the walls of their rooms.

Looking back over forty years of Harris's art, as assembled by the Art Gallery of Toronto in 1948, one notices how many failures as well as successes are to be met with in his work. His career as a painter was not always one of steady progress. Occasionally he fell into a too facile formula of simplification, at other times he handled shapes and contours with almost geometrical rigidity, while more than once he used what an unfavourable critic has called " blancmange colouring." But he has never let any such failures dominate him for long, and one can readily forget them before the simple majesty of his greater and better known pictures. In the best of them, as in *Bylot Island* (Plate VI), he has always attained an easy sureness in his depiction of massive forms. In this canvas, done following a summer voyage to Greenland and Baffin Island in 1930, he has been able to suggest the unrelenting immensity of space in these far northern regions ; here, too, he manages to evoke that clear but fragile light which pervades and penetrates the upper distances of the Arctic in summer, while at the same time it leaves a menacing darkness beneath in valleys and on shadowed shores.

On the whole, he has sought to tame the chaos of Nature, to fit it into the mould of his own thought. Yet, to-day, he has given up, or at least temporarily dropped, these struggles to impose his own conceptions of formal order upon the visible world.

He now concentrates instead upon non-objective compositions, in many of which he claims he is trying to give " statements of ideas and intimations of a philosophic kind in plastic, æsthetic and emotive terms." To some of his followers these have a mystical appeal, but, generally speaking, to many friendly observers they appear to be, as one critic recently described them, " The art of a Puritan who, by the rigorous imposition of theory, strives to create some kind of metaphysical ecstasy in paint."

F. H. VARLEY (1881-   )

A Fusion of the Lyrical and the Mystical

THAT talented Yorkshireman, Fred Varley, who had gone as a young man from his home town of Sheffield to study at the Académie Royale des Beaux-Arts in Antwerp and who had then spent " several years illustrating in London and several years drifting in the underworld," the details of which, he added, were " all right for a novel, but altogether unprintable as autobiography," must have found the atmosphere of Toronto, to which he migrated early in 1912, rather tame at first. In those days, this city was still maintaining a reputation for the solidity of its virtues, a reputation which was reflected in even the most radical of its painters, whom he now met through his friend Arthur Lismer.

To these new Canadian colleagues of his, " la vie de bohême " held no attractions whatsoever. Being artists who earned their living by working in commercial engraving plants and advertising offices, they had to stick closely to art-room desks during the week ; so they made at once for the countryside on Saturdays and Sundays. They organised excursions to nearby lakes and rivers, where they sketched in oils or sometimes went fishing. They now tried to convince Varley, who was more interested in painting people than jack pine, that the main and the most truly Canadian subject to portray was the Canadian northland. Varley resisted this trend for a while, but not for long. The spirit of this new movement in Canadian art was contagious and soon he, too, was going on the occasional camping trip to Georgian Bay. In 1920 he produced, for exhibition in one of the first Group of Seven shows, a large canvas, *Georgian Bay*, which, with its broad sweep of wave and wind and sky, has now become a favourite among visitors to the National Gallery in Ottawa. Yet this emphasis placed by the Group on rugged northern scenes was never really, at heart, accepted by him, and his best work continued to be then, as it always has been, portraiture or figures related to landscape.

While he was, of all those in the Group of Seven, the one whose work was the least dogmatically regionalist in conviction, his eyes, nevertheless, remained constantly in tune with his environment. For example, he had not long been in Canada before he discarded the brownish tones which had characterised his painting of the earlier Beaux-Arts days. In the end he became " the most luminous of the Seven in his handling of pigment, par-

VII. F. H. VARLEY, A.R.C.A. (1881-   )
"Vera"

Oil: 23½″ × 19½″.   The Right Hon. Vincent Massey, C.H., Port Hope, Ontario

ticularly in his greens, a colour which the others never saw in such varied lights."

Much of his best work was done after 1926. In that year he took a teaching post at the Vancouver School of Art and moved to the West Coast of Canada to live.

" British Columbia is heaven," he wrote in a letter to a friend in Halifax. " It trembles within me and pains with its wonder as when a child I first awakened to the song of the earth at home. Only the hills are bigger, the torrents are bigger. The sea is here, and the sky is as vast ; and humans— little bits of mind—would clamber up rocky slopes, creep in and out of mountain passes, fish in the streams, build little hermit cabins in sheltered places, curl up in sleeping bags and sleep under the stars. The Japanese fish, Chinese have vegetable gardens, Hindoos haul wood, and I often feel that only the Chinese of the eleventh and twelfth century ever interpreted the spirit of such a country. We have not yet awakened to its nature."

The longer he stayed in Vancouver—he remained there for ten years— the more his imagination was moved by the mystical qualities of the landscape and by its contrast or relationship to those " humans—little bits of mind," who dwelt within its overshadowing confines. There is an oil painting of his (now in the Art Gallery of Toronto) of a girl who, sitting on the rude porch of a cottage, looks up in meditation upon the mountains about her. This composition, through its title, *Dhârâna*, a Buddhist term signifying the power to project oneself into one's surroundings, reveals the clue to the problems which were occupying his mind at that time.

As an artist he had always been versatile. But in British Columbia, the range of his expression now became greater than before. A large number of drawings, water-colours, small oil studies on wooden panels and larger canvases, both of people and scenery, stand as the solid fruits of his accomplishment during the decade he spent on the Pacific Coast. His best drawings of this period are more than mere sketches ; they are works of art in themselves. In a few, those showing deep timbered valleys and rocky hillsides, he combines an almost Chinese economy and fluidity of statement with a keen observation of the details of bushes, trees and rocks. This power of suggestion is even more noticeable in some of his water-colours. In the one illustrated, *Mountain Lake* (Plate 26), the washes, which he has brushed in over the lines of the drawing, evoke the atmosphere of the scene and give us something of its predominant mood ; as far as drawing is concerned, it is based on only the slightest of hints, a few lines which mean trees, a few more for a mountain and others for a lake. Varley has in fact surpassed all other Canadian artists of his generation in his ability to depict the less austere and more mysterious moods of Canadian nature in water-colours of great delicacy, in which he merges acute perception with a high degree of simplification.

43

Partly from ideas picked up in his reading and partly from his own mystical qualities of observation, Varley many years ago became convinced that certain colours could be linked directly to the expression of psychology and character and should so be used in portrait painting. " Green," he says, is a " spiritual colour," the colours of the earth are " lusty," pale violet is " æsthetic " and so forth. He also believes that " colour vibrations, emanating from the object portrayed," enter into the maze of light and colour already present about " the object portrayed " and that this relationship has to be carefully analysed and mastered before one can hope to complete a satisfactory portrait. This analysis becomes all the more essential, he adds, if one wishes to link the personality of the sitter to the surrounding mood of time and place. His personal use of colour appears in some of his finest works, such as *Vera* (Plate VII), and the more recent *Portrait of Dr. T.* (Plate 25). Sometimes the application of these theories of his, however, provide more perplexing results, as in that controversial and misunderstood canvas, *Liberation*, which is on the theme of the resurrection.

It also has meant that families who were asked to accept, in portraits, pink as the predominant aura of colour surrounding their father and bread-winner, or wives who saw no purple investing the radiance of their husbands, have scorned the results of Varley's labours and have called his pictures caricatures of reality. But usually it is the families who have been wrong. Varley tends to sense, only too well, those qualities of strength or fallacies of character which are in the sitter, and, aided by his choice of colours, he emphasises with equal honesty both flaws and virtues. But it is not in this way that fashionable portrait commissions are won or a steady income obtained from clients.

Although an inspiring teacher who has always been able to arouse interest and enthusiasm among his students, Varley, nevertheless, after he left Vancouver in 1936, found it difficult at first to re-establish himself in eastern Canada. For a few years he was in charge of classes being held by the Ottowa Art Association, but the outbreak of war in 1939 made it necessary for that organisation to cancel its programme of activities and Varley was left without a job. He did manage, however, one summer about this time to be taken along as an artist on the Government-owned supply ship, the *Beothic*, on its annual voyage to the Canadian Arctic, and he brought back from this trip a remarkable series of water-colours and a few oil sketches. Afterwards, in Montreal and then in Toronto, he existed for a while on the most meagre of resources—a few sales of sketches each year and one or two portrait commissions at the most. But with the assistance of friends and patrons in Toronto, he has now managed to put these difficult days of the immediate past behind him. Dealers and collectors are taking more interest than ever before in his paintings and drawings. Also for a few years recently he taught at a small art school in the village of Doon. near Kitchener, Ontario.

To-day, as he approaches old age, he is given more than ever to reading translations of writings by Chinese authors. From these philosophers and poets he quotes phrases and verses concerning colour and equilibrium, abstruse references many of them, but related, he says, to much of the painting he is now doing.

SOME OTHERS IN THE GROUP OF SEVEN

MANITOBA, with its brittle atmosphere in winter and its clear dry skies and flat horizons, presents many a difficult problem to those artists who seek to retain in their paintings any degree of subtlety. That Lionel LeMoine FitzGerald, in such works as *Williamson's Garage* (Plate 35), should have been able to capture effectively, within the confines of precise drawing and brushwork, this sharpness of winter sunlight falling upon buildings and snow, is a tribute to his ability to adapt his own personal refinements of technique to the exigencies of western landscape.

Returning to his native city of Winnipeg after taking advanced studies at the Art Students League in New York, FitzGerald was little known outside his own neighbourhood until the members of the Group of Seven came to notice and admire his paintings. Then, in 1931, he was invited to join the Group, and he exhibited with it during the last two years of its existence.

About this same time the Group added to its membership a figure painter from Montreal, Edwin Holgate, who had been accustomed to portray prospectors and lumberjacks in sturdy outline against forest backgrounds. But Holgate's best work is perhaps to be found among his less obvious examples of Canadiana, as in the portrait, *Ludovine* (Plate 34), or in *Coolie Girl, Jamaica*, now in the Provincial Museum of Quebec. In fact the nationalist movement, in so far as it spelled rock and pine and the cold waters of northern lakes, sometimes proved to be an unhappy influence in his work, particularly when he began to do compositions of studio nudes outlined against backdrops of clearly regional flora and Pre-Cambrian geological outcroppings. These fortunately turned out to be but passing accidents in his career, and of late he has avoided all such extremes of regionalist enthusiasm.

As for FitzGerald, he worked too slowly and painstakingly ever to be affected by such vagaries of fashion as those which so disturbed Holgate. He painted little, and that little with precise care. Most of his year was given over to his duties as principal of the Winnipeg School of Art. The relatively few water-colours and oils he did of the prairie or of the thin tracery of trees along the edges of Manitoba streams were, however, always much admired, as were also his more numerous drawings.

In 1943 he began going to Bowen Island near Vancouver to spend his summers, and in this new environment he did first a series of monochrome drawings and then some water-colours of a minute delicacy. His friend Lawren Harris wrote of them : " One water-colour pictures a railing and a great weather-vane trellis which FitzGerald devised and made himself and

VIII. EMILY CARR (1871-1945)
"Blunden Harbour"

Oil: 51″ × 37″. *National Gallery of Canada, Ottawa*

which pictured against the water and sky and mountains makes a resonant and supernal symbol of the spirit of the Pacific Coast. Somehow it embodies the feeling of the Indians, the feeling of the woods and skies and the West Coast fiords. Other paintings are of the upper reaches of the mountains across from Bowen Island with their peaks in the summer clouds and the clouds around and above the mountains, at once caressing and soaring and remote."

FitzGerald has now retired from teaching and gone permanently to the West Coast to dwell. Some of his latest water-colours seem too coolly intellectual, and at the same time too evanescent in detail and technique, to appeal to most of his previous followers. Yet, partly because of their very negation of emotionalism in line and colour, they appear to be highly regarded by others, who, like Lawren Harris, feel that FitzGerald has achieved in them " an utter simplicity of mood and dignity of spirit."

Before its disbandment in 1932, the Group of Seven had reached a total of nine members. In addition to MacDonald, Jackson, Harris, Lismer, Varley, FitzGerald and Holgate, there were also Franklin Carmichael and A. J. Casson. The oils and water-colours of northern Ontario landscapes which Carmichael painted, while interesting enough within the limitations of his style, never did possess anything like the same variety or power as was to be found in the best productions of MacDonald, Harris or Jackson. Casson, after he joined the Group in 1926, became fairly well known for his tidy but angular renderings of the unadorned architecture of Ontario villages, which scenes he usually bathed in a somewhat unreal and rigid light, as if they were isolated settings on a stage. He also went to northern Ontario for his subjects, and some of his water-colours of Lake Superior, because of their greater spontaneity of execution, are preferred by some to his oils. To-day, he is the capable art director of a prominent firm which specialises in fine colour reproductions and silk-screen printing. He is also president of the Royal Canadian Academy, to which distinguished post he was elected in 1946.

EMILY CARR (1871-1945)

An Expressionist among the Totem Poles

IN France, about the year 1905, those younger artists who were seeking a freer way of painting founded the Salon d'Automne. Matisse, Derain, Segonzac were among the constant supporters of this salon. One Canadian, James Wilson Morrice, also found a place among its talented company, and in one of his letters, dated August 1910, he states : " I am working like a slave now for the Salon d'Automne, which opens next month. It is the most interesting exhibition of the year—somewhat revolutionary at times, but it has the most original work."

What a surprise then to read in her autobiography, *Growing Pains*, which was published posthumously, a similar passage written by Emily Carr ! Certainly few had thought previously of this strange and isolated regional painter from British Columbia in terms of Paris or of those exciting days before the First Great War when France was the unchallenged centre of individual expression and experiment in art. Yet, writing of the year 1911, when she was in France, she recalls : " I had two canvases accepted and well hung in the Salon d'Automne (the rebel Paris show of the year)."

In her own book, she reveals her authentic background. From her earliest youth she knew what she wanted to do, that was to paint, and as soon as she had finished high school in Victoria, the small city on Vancouver Island where she was born, she persuaded her guardian (her mother and father were dead) to allow her to attend art school in San Francisco (that was about 1888) ; then she moved on to the Westminster School of Art in London. Some years afterwards, using money she herself had earned by teaching art in Vancouver, she went to Paris. In these travels her health suffered and her doctors several times told her she must no longer work in these crowded cities. Yet despite such difficulties, she persisted in her studies abroad. For instance, concerning her work in Canada in the period 1904-10, after her return home from London, she writes : " I had learned a lot from the Indians, but who except Canadians themselves could help me comprehend her great woods and spaces. San Francisco had not, London had not. What about this New Art Paris talked of ? It claimed bigger broader seeing . . ."

So she went to Paris, not for the sake of Paris, but to be able to paint Indian villages better. She studied at Colarossi's, a studio to which young students from all over the world flocked. She also went to Concarneau, where she appears to have studied for a while in classes given by Frances Hodgkins, the New Zealand artist who achieved fame afterwards in England. But her principal teacher was Harry Gibb,[1] a painter from England who ran

[1] Henry Phelan Gibb, who was a friend of Gertrude Stein and an early admirer of Matisse and Picasso.

17. TOM THOMSON (1877-1917)
"Northern River"
Oil: 45″ × 40″.   National Gallery of Canada, Ottawa

18.   TOM THOMSON (1877-1917)
"The West Wind"
Oil: 47" × 53".   Art Gallery of Toronto

19. TOM THOMSON (1877-1917)
" Edge of the Log Run "
Oil sketch on wooden panel: 8½″ × 10½″. Mrs. H. A. Dyde, Edmonton

20. J. E. H. MacDONALD, R.C.A. (1873-1932)
" Cattle by the Creek "
Oil: 26″ × 32″. National Gallery of Canada, Ottawa

21. J. E. H. MacDONALD, R.C.A. (1873-1932)
" October Shower Gleam "
Oil: 44″ × 49½″. Hart House, University of Toronto

22. J. E. H. MacDONALD, R.C.A. (1873-1932)
" Goat Range, Rocky Mountains "
Oil: 20½″ × 25½″. Mrs. H. P. de Pencier, Toronto

23. ARTHUR LISMER, R.C.A. (1885-   )
" October on the North Shore "
Oil: 48″ × 64″. National Gallery of Canada, Ottawa

24. ARTHUR LISMER, R.C.A. (1885-   )
" The *Olympic* with Returned Soldiers "
Oil: 48" × 64". Canadian War Memorials Collection, National Gallery of Canada, Ottawa

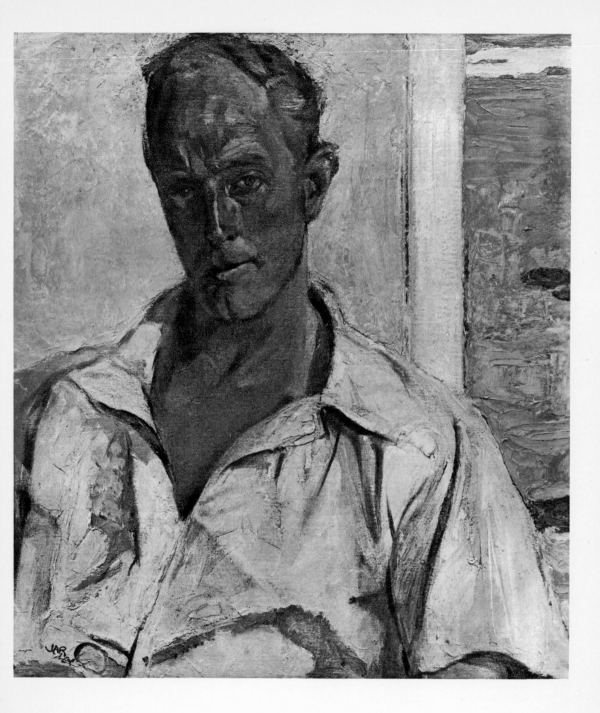

25. F. H. VARLEY, A.R.C.A. (1881-   )
" Portrait of Dr. T., 1945 "
Oil: 22⅝″ × 20½″. C. S. Band, Esq., Toronto

26. F. H. VARLEY, A.R.C.A. (1881-   )
"Mountain Lake"
Water-colour: 11½″ × 14″. *National Gallery of Canada, Ottawa*

27. LAWREN HARRIS (1885-   )
"Shacks"
Oil: 42″ × 50½″.   National Gallery of Canada, Ottawa

28.   LAWREN HARRIS (1885-   )
" Afternoon Sun, Lake Superior "
Oil: 40½″ × 50½″.   National Gallery of Canada, Ottawa

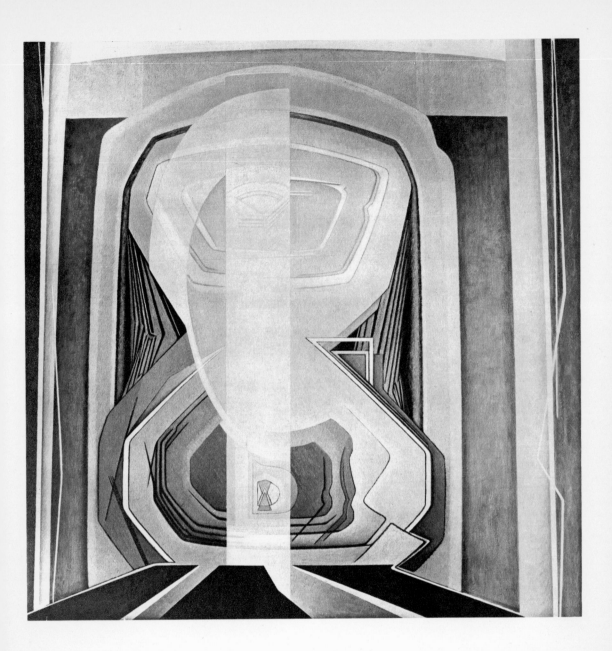

29.   LAWREN HARRIS (1885-   )
"Abstract Composition"
Oil: 60" × 60".   National Gallery of Canada, Ottawa

30.   EMILY CARR (1871-1945)
"Indian Church"
Oil: 42¼″ × 26¾″. C. S. Band, Esq., Toronto

31. EMILY CARR (1871-1945)
" Landscape, Trees "
Oil: 36" × 24". Mrs. Duncan Campbell Scott, Ottawa

32. **EMILY CARR** (1871-1945)
" Landscape "
Oil: 22″ × 34″. National Gallery of Canada, Ottawa

his own classes and who looked with favour on the sketches of Indian life she had brought from Canada. " He was convinced as I that the new art was going to help my work out west, show me a bigger way of approach."

Her more advanced work, however, met with neither sympathy nor recognition, when, after returning to British Columbia late in 1911, she tried to paint Canada with this " bigger way of approach." Back in Vancouver, she even lost the few pupils she had. This does not mean that her fellow-citizens alone were to blame. The whole state of art appreciation everywhere in Canada was most backward at that time. Had she been in Montreal, she would not have been much better off, for, a few years later, the news-papers and art critics of that city were to launch a bitter and sustained attack upon the work of several independent Canadian painters, including John Lyman, who had returned in 1913 from Paris. The attack of the critics was directed against all examples of modern art, Canadian or otherwise, and was summed up by S. Morgan-Powell, the Montreal art pundit of the day, when he wrote : " They convince one that those responsible for them can neither draw nor compose nor colour." That, too, was precisely what Vancouver thought of Emily Carr.

Her relatives also took the same attitude. One of her sisters told her : " It is crazy to persist in this way—no pupils, no sales, you'll starve ! Go back to the old painting." But she replied : " I'd rather starve ! I could not paint in the old way—it is dead—meaningless—empty."

To earn her living she now returned to Victoria, where she began to make pottery to sell to tourists. " I could bake as many as 500 pieces at one firing." She raised Old English Bobtail sheep-dogs and, at one stage, she turned her home into a " Ladies' Boarding House," where she was forced to listen in patience while " these creatures—my bread and butter—jeered at my pictures on the wall, jeered before my very nose."

Of that period she writes : " I never painted now—had neither time nor wanting. For about fifteen years I did not paint."

For fifteen years, years in which the art of James Wilson Morrice was reaching its richest maturity, in which A. Y. Jackson and Lawren Harris and J. E. H. MacDonald were busily engaged in founding a new school of Canadian landscape painting, during all these years she did not once lift her brush to canvas. That was the tragedy which was to cast its shadow over her whole life.

Those were long, sullen, repressed years. Yet, eventually, they came to an end. Dr. Marius Barbeau and Mortimer Lamb both showed interest in her paintings of Indian villages and visited her in Victoria. There, too, came Eric Brown, Director of the National Gallery of Canada. The National Gallery then borrowed fifty of her canvases to put in a show of West Coast Indian Art in Ottawa in 1927 ; she also was invited to visit Toronto and Ottawa. On her trip east, she found people—artists, Canadians—had become interested in her paintings. She met the members of the Group of Seven in Toronto ; they proved to be most cordial and friendly. " Here everyone was so kind that I wanted to run away and hide, yet I did want, too, to hear what they said of my work. I had not heard anything nice about it since I left France."

So began the renaissance, the revival of her spirit. From 1927 on she set to work, with intense concentration, to paint the forest landscapes of her native province. To be sure, she had continuing moments of loneliness and depression, but she fought her way through them, assisted to a great extent by the encouragement she received from Lawren Harris.

A foreboding dread, a fear almost of Nature and its power, comes out in such brooding compositions as *Indian Church* (Plate 30), with its white church overshadowed, overawed, as it were, by contorted columns of spruce and fir. Those columns are partly decorative, as the formalised rocks and trees of Lawren Harris were decorative, but they pass beyond mere decoration. The whole pattern of her forest becomes so dramatic, so contorted with moody content, that you can, without straining your imagination, readily visualise certain formal resemblances to the dark shadows and the bold reliefs of Spanish baroque cathedrals.

We need only read Miss Carr's own book of essays, *Klee Wyck*, to find out what are some of the more primitive meanings attributed to Nature which she attempts to call up in her paintings. As literature, her interpretations of Indian legends and her accounts, realistic but weird, of the life and the unspoken dreads of the Indian tribes who inhabit those mountain-shadowed inlets, are often brilliantly conceived.

By using a sort of covered trailer or van outfitted for housekeeping, Emily Carr was able, after 1933, despite periods of failing health, to go camping at the edge of the forest when and as she wished. There, in the shadow of some immense grove of evergreens, she used to spend her time " painting with great rapidity all day and, at night, closed up in the solitude of the van, reading Walt Whitman and writing."

In the paintings she did during the last years of her life, the darkness of the forest is lessened. The tense, brooding forms are gone. The subjects are now sunlit patches, open slopes of burned-over land or waves beating against a sandy beach, with the forest in the background. In these she becomes even joyful at times. Some will like the austerity of her earlier compositions better ; others prefer the happy freedom of her later works.

What is certain is that her controlled exuberance of drawing, her use of the strokes and outlines of the brush to create coherence and pattern, also her tendency to design with colour as well as with contour, enable her to be ranked, apart from any purely regional significance which may be attributed to her, as an original painter possessed of a strong sense of organic construction in design.

IX.   PRUDENCE HEWARD (1896-1947)
"The Farmer's Daughter"
Oil: 24″×20″.   *National Gallery of Canada, Ottawa*

PRUDENCE HEWARD (1896-1947)

Personal Realism in Portraiture

PRUDENCE HEWARD of Montreal was never at any time a prolific painter. Hers was a slow development. Yet during the last ten years or so of her career she did a number of sturdily gay and brightly coloured figure compositions and portraits, with highly rhythmic landscape backgrounds, which possess considerable power. One of the best of these, *The Farmer's Daughter*, is reproduced as Plate IX.

Following her untimely death in 1947, at the age of 51, whole-hearted appreciations of her achievements were recorded in memorial notices written by Edwin Holgate, who had been one of her fellow-students years before under William Brymner at the Art Association classes in Montreal, and by A. Y. Jackson, who had often gone sketching with her and her friends in the Ontario countryside.

" There was nothing very revolutionary or controversial about her work," Jackson wrote in his introduction to the memorial exhibition organised by the National Gallery of Canada in 1948, " nor was there even very much of it—a span of sixteen years covers almost her entire creative period and much of this time was lost through illness." He added : " She held no narrow nationalistic views on art, yet had little sympathy with those who belittled everything which had its roots in our own soil." As to the development of her work, he described this clearly in the following paragraphs :

" When she won the Willingdon Arts Competition in 1929, Prudence Heward was scarcely known as an artist even in Montreal. The prize-winning picture, *Girl on a Hill*,[1] was bold in design and was painted with much assurance. From that time onward she showed a steady and consistent development until 1945, when illness made it impossible for her to continue. Most of her canvases were painted at the Heward house on Peel Street in Montreal where she used a room on the top floor as a studio. Here her young nieces posed for many of the pictures, though she occasionally used a model. She did not find it easy to paint : she was not " clever." Her usual procedure was to use one of her landscape sketches as the background for a figure piece. She liked working on large canvases, and she would struggle, with many misgivings, for fullness of form and bold contrasts of colour. There were some failures, but much to learn from them ; and such works as *Rollande*, *Clytie*,

---

[1] In the collection of The National Gallery of Canada, Ottawa.

Dark Girl, Farmhouse Window and the portraits of her nieces Efa and Barbara, revealed her as an artist of real distinction. Though she was chiefly interested in figure painting, she also painted flowers, still life and many landscape studies.

" The out-of-doors sketches represent what were probably the happiest days of her life. Most of them were painted at Fernbank, the family's summer home on the bank of the St. Lawrence near Brockville. Here the green water of the river flowed through the Thousand Islands and a continuous succession of boats passed a few hundred yards from the shore . . . It was typical lower Ontario country, flat for the most part but with the rock cropping out through the shallow soil. The sketching was done around such old settlements as Tincap, Lynn and Ballycanoe ; the subjects were weather-beaten barns and silos, little wooden churches, pasture fields and the scattered wood lots with their pines, maples and elms.

" In Montreal, Prudence worked in close collaboration with her friend Sarah.[1] The big house on Peel Street was a centre for artists to gather. The Canadian Group of Painters, of which she was for a time vice-president, often met there. She was devoted to her artist friends and was keenly interested in all the developments of art. To one of her friends she once said that if she could not paint she did not want to live. Though shy and reserved in public, she was respected by her friends for her sincerity and for the quiet, persuasive way in which she expressed her ideas. She had plenty of time to consider and plan her course through all the conflicting ideologies which tend to confuse the artists of to-day. From the *Girl on a Hill* to her last painting there was no change in intention, but only a continuous effort to realise that intention more fully, to express it more perfectly.

" Like most young Canadian painters she had great admiration for the moderns, such as Cézanne, Renoir, Matisse, Derain, Picasso, Modigliani and, among others, Frances Hodgkins, two of whose paintings she was proud to possess. But their influence did not mean imitation, for she was content to be herself. The appreciation of fellow-artists and such recognition as one could receive in Canada satisfied any desire which she had for fame."

Towards the end of her career she concentrated upon portrait studies, but occasionally she returned to the more direct treatment of landscape. When she did so, as in this delightful picture, *A Summer Day* (Plate 36), one sees at once how much broader and more sustained her powers of imagination now were than they had been before in her earlier and more derivative out-door sketches. This composition is based on the view of the St. Lawrence River as seen from the porch of her family's summer home. In its freedom of conception, it recalls those flowing designs of Frances Hodgkins, in which objects of still life and landscape, foreground and background, mingle in one harmonious whole. But one would be wrong to trace too close a con-

[1] Sarah Robertson (1891-1948), a Montreal Painter.

nection between her final work and that of this New Zealand artist, settled in England, whose paintings she so much admired. After all, as Edwin Holgate said in the memorial tribute he paid to Prudence Heward, while " her taste and appreciation covered a wide range," yet at the same time her mature painting always " remained constant to her own personal idiom."

PARASKEVA CLARK (1898-   )

An Honest Sophistication

"I NEVER dreamed of being an artist at all until I came to Canada," Paraskeva Clark once declared. This statement of hers, while in a sense true, is yet something of an enthusiastic exaggeration, for she did possess a considerable background of art training before she arrived in Canada in 1931. As a girl, she had painted in Leningrad, where she was born, and had gone to art classes there until shortly before her departure for Paris in 1923. On the other hand, it is true that while working in France—for part of the time she was a salesgirl in a shop—she had few or no opportunities to take up her brush again. But when her Canadian husband brought her to Toronto to live, she was so delighted with the pleasant surroundings of her home, the foliage-covered ravines and the cultivated fields and woodlands of the adjoining countryside, that she now began to paint again in good earnest.

While she now gave herself over whole-heartedly to the Ontario scene, her devotion to it, however, was far from being naïve. She retained too many memories of her early European training—whether she is now willing to admit all these influences or not—to allow her to treat Ontario wheat-fields and lakes and country lanes with anything but a strictly personal refinement and perception. The qualities you most notice in her work, when you compare it with that of most other Canadian woman painters of her generation, many of whom still labour too much in the shadow of the Group of Seven, is " her delicate and evocative taste in colour, the way in which she may purposefully understate," which, as Andrew Bell explains in a tribute he recently paid her, " are all reflections of a good kind of sophistication—the almost spiritualised kind."

As for the impact of her arrival in Toronto, Pearl McCarthy summed this up amusingly enough in a newspaper article written in 1942, when she said : " About eleven years ago, people in Toronto were heard to ask, ' Who is that ? '—looking towards a young woman of unmistakable distinction. A few years later, people were heard to ask, ' Who painted that ? ' —looking at pictures of such distinctive character as called for either approval or resentment."

To answer the question " Who is that ? " one need only look at *Self-portrait* (Plate 37). This painting shows clearly how vital and nervous and strong her personality is. She sometimes refers to it as *Self-portrait with a Concert Programme*. This is because the leaflet in her hand was one for a " Salute to Russia " rally held during the war ; and her reason for dis-

54

X. DAVID MILNE (1882-   )
" The Saint "
Water-colour: 18″ × 22″. National Gallery of Canada, Ottawa

playing it thus was that, while being genuinely and outspokenly a Canadian, she at the same time wanted to stress her warm sympathy for her native land.

As for present-day Soviet painting, her point of view, as she gave it then in a public lecture, was that, while Russian art had frankly only reached the adolescent stage, it still should not be too hastily condemned in its present manifestations as Victorian, since the masses who received it liked it.

This problem of the relation of art to society is always with her. She defines her creed as follows : " Any nationally recognised artist is really working in the service of the national culture, with the unwritten pledge and moral obligation to devote all his abilities and knowledge to the development of art and to the promotion of greater art appreciation by the people. . . ."

Yet she never confuses in her work this kind of social purpose with any need to compromise or pander to vulgarisation of taste. She fights rather for the proper recognition and treatment of artists. For example, she has been advocating recently a reform in the handling of travelling exhibitions, whereby painters, by being paid a fee for works they loan, will be encouraged to send their very best work on tour of the smaller towns of the Dominion. She also is willing to take some of that precious time, which is left to her for her painting after she has finished her household tasks, and to use it in organisational duties connected with various art groups, such as the Canadian Society of Painters in Water Colour, of which she has been president.

There is one aspect of her painting which deserves underlining. This is her ability to grasp the wonders of her own backyard and neighbouring streets. As Andrew Bell observes in an essay he wrote in *Canadian Art* : " Many Canadian painters have failed to notice, or have preferred to ignore, because they sensed themselves discoverers of the Canadian land, the art at their doorstep. It has been quite otherwise with Paraskeva Clark. For her, the subjects crying out to be set down in formalised beauty are everywhere. She could not, as a wife and mother, move much about the country, but she could work up pictures of the intimate world close at hand. And so it has been in her portraits, studies in still life and to a large extent even in her landscapes. The portraits, and they are admirable, have been of her husband, her sons, close friends, or if none of these were about—then in seeming desperation, of herself. In still life, it has been an arrangement of familiar household objects, or of flowers or fish. In landscape, it is frequently a transcription of what chances to please her beyond one of her windows. *Our Street in Autumn* is an example. What a triumph in mood this picture is ! You know that urban street, and you have been inside those houses. You recognise as incontrovertibly true that brilliant, yet mellow, autumn colour."

Concerning her early training, she writes : " I was born in Leningrad and worked under Vassily Schoukaeff and Kuzma Petrov-Vodkin in the Free Studios in the former Academy of Arts . . . You see, the Academy was disbanded in 1918 by the Soviet Government and in its place were opened so-called Free Studios where the best artists, of all varied art movements, were invited to teach and where anybody could enrol even without any knowledge of art . . . and according to individual taste and choice." Her choice must have been for those painters who had been influenced by French art, from the post-impressionists onwards, for she shows herself to be clearly influenced by their method of using colour to define form. This is apparent in all her landscapes. There is also a certain structural power in her portraits which derives from some knowledge of the earlier periods of cubism. The arrangement of space and the assembly of line and colour in her paintings of people seems to be allied to those techniques developed by Picasso before 1910, but she did not obtain them directly from French sources, if we are to accept her own explanation.

She has stated her position as an artist as follows : " I am a realist. But the experience of being deeply moved, being spellbound, comes to me only while looking at the miraculous creations of modern masters. My teacher, Kuzma Petrov-Vodkin, wrote a book—the *Euclid's Space*—in which to his pupils he gave a compass for finding the way in the maze of Nature's complicated and deceiving aspects. He said : ' Look for the eternal truth of a sphere, of a cone, or a cube. . . .' In all humility, I am trying."

CHARLES COMFORT (1900-   ) and W. A. OGILVIE (1901-   )

The Adjustment to Society

DURING the early nineteen-thirties in Toronto, as the economic slump deepened, those younger artists, whose talents seemed destined to bring them at least a moderate success as easel painters, began to view with some apprehension the road which lay before them. Material problems, such as how to pay the next month's rent, confronted them at every turn ; doubts about the spiritual content of their art also assailed them. In what sense, they wondered, had their previous urge to paint northern landscape been merely a romantic escape ? Could a more honest realism be found in the depiction of city slums ? Had their great error been one of neglecting humanity itself ? Some of them might have wished to return to " art for art's sake " as a solution, but this was manifestly impossible without a private income, and none of them were so fortunate as to possess one. To be sure, there were usually a few teaching posts available, but these had become rarer during depression years. As for jobs in commercial art, most engraving plants and studios were now dismissing employees, not hiring them. Certainly there was no one easy answer. Some artists forsook painting entirely ; others struggled along in poverty or, like David Milne, took to a hermit's existence in the woods. But was it necessary to go to such extremes ? Was it not possible to make some workable compromise with the stern facts of the material world ?

Two friends who used to talk over these problems were Charles Comfort and Will Ogilvie. The former had been born in Scotland and brought up as a boy in Winnipeg ; the latter was a newcomer from South Africa, who had only recently arrived in Canada. Both of them had previously taken advanced training at the Art Students League in New York. But now in 1932 they had to give up for the moment any immediate ambitions they might have had for themselves in the realms of pure art. The problem was no longer one of personal expression in painting but rather how to get and keep a job and earn one's board and keep. One way out, they decided, was to fight the slump together as partners ; this they would do by going into business on their own, by setting up a studio which would accept any type of commission available, from portraiture to advertising layout, from architectural decoration to magazine illustration. So that year, joining with another artist named Ayres, they pooled their resources of talent, took an office and went out to seek business. In spite of, or maybe because of, their diverse backgrounds, they managed to do reasonably well as a firm. Also, they were able to ration out the hours in which they would do their own painting, and they found they had time enough, too, to go on sketching trips during the summer.

Comfort, in particular, wandered as far afield as Nova Scotia, the Saguenay River in Quebec and the North Shore of Lake Superior. During these years, he also succeeded in developing his craft as a muralist, when he did large panels for both the North American Life building and the Toronto Stock Exchange. Then he went on to widen his emotional range as an artist by painting large portraits in water-colour which were remarkable for their breadth and vigour. This can be seen from his portrait of Carl Schaefer, which has, as Robert Ayre has said, " a robustness to be found nowhere else in Canadian water-colour painting, achieving on a large paper, thirty-six by forty, the massiveness of an oil, while retaining the spontaneity of the other medium." Comfort gave it the title, *Young Canadian* (Plate 38). Conveying as it did both perplexity and repressed strength, this painting seemed, to many at the time, to symbolise the state of mind of Canadian youth during the difficult depression years. It was bought by Hart House, that recreational and cultural centre for men students at the University of Toronto.

Hart House also commissioned Ogilvie to do murals for its chapel. These murals of his, when completed in 1936, were described as " a commingling of youth and the spiritual in the broadest manner," in which Ogilvie took " his inspiration partly from primitive Italian altar-pieces and partly from the formal aspects of Canadian landscape."

The commercial partnership between the two men came to an end in 1936 when Ogilvie went to the Art Association School in Montreal to teach. In the same year, Comfort became a teacher of mural painting at the Ontario College of Art, and in 1938 he joined the staff of the Department of Fine Art at the University of Toronto. To teach for a salary and to paint for oneself in one's spare time was a common enough way of life for most established artists in Canada, and now it looked as if these two men had made up their minds that this, too, was the kind of life into which they fitted best. But they had barely settled down into it when war broke out.

Once before, in 1932, they had shown themselves capable of meeting changed circumstances with frankness and fortitude. Both of them now faced the stern realities of war as directly as they had tackled once before the problems of the slump. Comfort enlisted in 1941 in the Reserve Officers' Training Corps and Ogilvie went overseas the same year in the Duke ol York's Royal Canadian Hussars. After training in England, Ogilvie was promoted from the ranks to become a lieutenant and an official war artist. Later he became a captain and then a major. In 1946 he was awarded the M.B.E. for his achievement in recording, often under enemy fire, the landings and the advance of the Canadian Army in Italy.

" The first significant work by a Canadian war artist in an active theatre of war was done by Capt. W. A. Ogilvie of Montreal," wrote Comfort, who by now in 1944 had also become a war artist and a major with the Canadian Army in Italy. " Ogilvie waded ashore from the landing barges on Pachino Beach in the invasion of Sicily and has made a stirring visual record of the Canadian action throughout the Sicilian campaign, the invasion of Italy, and the march up through the peninsula. He has produced a tremendous volume of sketches and notes, many made from vehicles on the move, nearly all made under fire."

Before the fighting ended, a total of ten painters had been appointed as official war artists in the Army. While their output was both varied and valuable, none of them brought back from the European fronts a more sincere and at the same time a more representative group of drawings than did Ogilvie. His productions, while documentary, still possessed a sensitivity of line and a certain easy grace in composition which was not too far removed from the work he had done previously in Canada. On the other hand, in content and emotion there was a great difference between those delicately drawn figures of draped women or of nude bathers, arranged in harmonious but yet restrained patterns, which he used to do during the nineteen-thirties, and these war sketches of dead horses and wrecked vehicles, choking and blocking the roads of Normandy, which he now made amid the smoke and deafening gunfire of battle.

As it happened, he was not always able to transcribe these drawings into oils of equal power. Removed from the immediate impact of these scenes, he seemed to lose emotional contact with them. For example, that large painting in the Canadian War Collection, *Escape Route, Falaise Gap*, based on his sketches, is as cold and straightforward as any poster.

But sometimes the oils, too, were successful, as in the one illustrated here of *Bombed Houses, Caen* (Plate 40). While there are no people in this composition and only the death of buildings is rendered, one cannot readily forget the haunting quality of these gaunt walls.

Besides these grimmer notes of war, he portrayed many of its duller and more homely aspects also, as when, in Italy, he employed as a recurrent motif in his drawings those groups of mules used by the Army to carry supplies over the mountain passes of the Apennines. In his hands, these mules and the soldiers with them became gentle expressive units, " reminiscent," as one fellow-artist wrote, " of Daumier's love of the unit of Don Quixote, Sancho Panza and their animals." His poignant depictions of refugees form an even more personal contribution. In these strongly realised yet sad and melancholy faces there is blackness and suffering, but also a gleam of desperate hope.

Comfort was more the omnivorous collector of data; he kept a voluminous diary when he was in Italy in which he recorded every moment of action and every new face or old monument seen. The water-colours and oils he did at the same time tended to be fairly work-a-day in feeling. Yet Comfort, in the midst of piling up information, occasionally obtained a fresh and spontaneous impression, very much alive, as is evident in such water-colours of his in the Canadian War Collection, as *Narrow Gauge Railway from Ortona to Orsogna, Italy*, where the calm beauty of the fields is broken by the tangled wreckage of a long line of electric power poles which run like a row of tattered gibbets across the landscape. He went everywhere to paint, from battlefields to churches; he did portraits of both generals and sergeants ; and visiting Rome he produced an impressive water-colour of a French-Canadian regiment attending mass in St. Peter's.

After 1946 the respite from the struggle of war appeared, for a while at least, to leave Ogilvie alone, turned in upon himself and prone to try to revive and create something once again out of his memories of the draped figures he had done so many years before. But this was only a passing phase; to-day he is obtaining an expression which is both sturdy and poetic, in his newer landscapes, particularly in those recent ones where groups of birds, wading or nesting on rocks, became the dominant feature of the composition.

Comfort was more quickly able to adjust himself and he turned readily to new experiments. On the whole, one **can** say of Comfort that he has an exploring mind, yet when he tries to do, as he has recently, more abstruse compositions, these attempts at abstraction often verge too much on showmanship. He has considerable talent and it is difficult sometimes for him not to play the virtuoso. As to what he is trying to do or say, his friend Robert Ayre has perhaps given the fairest appreciation. " Because he feels the need for understanding the complexities of our times, Comfort is an eclectic," Ayre writes, " and these new paintings may be taken as experiments towards an understanding of the newer ways of painting, an adventure into another experience. But Charles Comfort has not gone into the ivory tower and closed the door. He never will. He must communicate."

CARL SCHAEFER (1903-   )

Regional Painter of Rural Ontario

SOMBRE in content, yet illuminated here and there with broader passages of ochres and olives, the best of the paintings which Carl Schaefer did a few years ago, when he was an official war artist with the R.C.A.F., recall the tension of airfields at night, the flashing of revolving lights, the shadowed excitement of hurrying figures and the silhouettes of great planes hidden in the darkness.

Going through the bombings of London, he suffered shock, had his studio windows blown in and found painting impossible for long periods. Afterwards he had to shoulder his way through those various delays and barriers which seemed to beset every Canadian war artist, whether in the Air Force, Navy or Army, whenever they sought permission to do sketches near or under actual fighting conditions. Schaefer, however, did manage by sheer persistence to be assigned to many operational flights and he finally obtained 380 flying hours to his credit; also he saw, and participated in, more than one battle over London and the coast. From these he managed to acquire something of that direct emotional understanding of war in the air which he felt was essential to the making of any complete and fundamental record.

Yet while the paintings and drawings he brought back from Air Force stations in the United Kingdom and Iceland rank high in the archives of Canadian war art, his previous water-colours of rural scenery in western Ontario still remain his most characteristic achievement. His best work is a distinct form of regional art, presented, not with dramatic realism, but in a dry, reticent style. In his post-war paintings, his approach remains much the same, although now he often selects one thing, such as a stump or a few tangled weeds, and lets them tell their own story without reference to the broader panorama of field and meadow and sky.

From his first teachers, the Group of Seven, he obtained his early inspiration and purpose. But he preferred to forget the more severe strains of their nationalism and to concentrate, not on the northern wilderness, but on the cultivated pastures and tidy woodlots and well-worn country roads of his native Bruce and Grey counties in western Ontario. He brought to these subjects a sharp and far from sentimental vision. There was no emphasis here upon cows and sheep or rays of sunlight filtering through groves of maple and oak. The bucolic notes of the more orthodox painters were gone ; in their place was a new, an almost angular documentation. He did water-colours of a cross-roads cemetery or of an isolated schoolhouse, of a deserted shack with a weed-infested yard, or, by way of contrast, of the flower-bordered lawn and curved fretwork eaves of some prosperous late-Victorian farmhouse.

At first he had a few mannerisms of style, as when clumps of trees were made to look like the tops of brooms, but generally, as when he painted a small stretch of rail fence or a few stooks of wheat, as in this picture, *Stooks on John Voelzing's Farm* (Plate 39), his work was altogether unaffected, without pretence or show.

His drawing for a while retained a certain rudeness, but he was always striving to master greater freedom of draughtsmanship. To-day he has done so, and his ink and wash drawings possess a more original merit in their own right.

Although Schaefer does some oil paintings on canvas, the medium he always favoured until recently was water-colour.

You do not think of these water-colours of his in terms of courageous patterns. You admire them for other reasons. You dwell upon their mingled fluidity and crispness of drawing and their special use of colour, particularly to be noticed in the emphasis given to gay greens or harvest yellows. Finally, in looking back over the fine progression of paintings he did in the vicinity of his birthplace, the village of Hanover, you remember the " almost obstinate repetition of what might be thought commonplace subjects—frugal, profit-earning woodlots, broad but not limitless expanses of grain, scatterings of trees along the edge of a meadow, the monotonous roll of field and hillock in a pleasant but far from spectacular countryside." In them there is revealed, without the need of faces or the appearance of human figures, something of the inner psychology of the region, the atmosphere and sensibility of a solid and unassuming rural way of life.

Schaefer was the first Canadian artist to be awarded a Guggenheim Fellowship. This gave him the opportunity in 1940 for a year of complete freedom, to paint and study as he pleased anywhere in the United States. He was, at the beginning of that period, experimenting with new types of water-colour compositions, mostly of still life. When he obtained the scholarship, he did not, however, go to the metropolitan centres to immerse himself in studies and galleries. Instead, choosing a spot similar to the countryside he had always frequented, he settled down for a year in a hamlet on the banks of the Connecticut River in Vermont, and there his style slowly matured. Upon his return, he was given a commission as a war artist with the R.C.A.F. and his overseas experiences began. These duties with the war records were finally completed in 1946.

To-day he is established once again in southern Ontario, where he teaches art in Toronto. There and in nearby cities he often paints brooding compositions of some of the grimmer urban buildings ; one remembers several of gaol walls and another of a fortress-like penitentiary. But this proclivity for bleak and forbidding architecture deserts him when he returns to the old familiar scenes of the countryside, which he still depicts with sympathy, although often, in these as well as in his newer paintings of the city, he uses a heavier medium of oil combined with tempera, which gives an unusual opaqueness to much of his recent work. His best productions remain so far, beyond a doubt, those which he still does in water-colour with the same dry but sparkling simplicity as before.

DAVID MILNE (1882-   )

The Æsthetic Response

FOR years David Milne lived alone in the woods of Muskoka in a tiny hut, which was protected from the elements only by a few strips of tar paper. But he was content. Although his income was meagre, he still had enough to pay for oils and canvas and for paper and paint for his watercolours. On arriving by canoe to visit him in his isolated abode, you would be welcomed by him warmly ; then, given the chance, he would talk about art and criticism, about books and exhibitions, and go on to relate his memories of the great paintings he had seen years before in New York and Europe.

When he had reached the peak of his enthusiasm, he would speak in praise of John Constable, who had produced " art one could really believe in." " Not, mind you," he would continue, " Constable's heavy painting, his large gallery pictures "—and he would pause to mention how Constable had lived in a society weighed down with the desire for material possessions and had tried to conform to it by exhibiting canvases made to Academy measurements—" but those little sketches that he produced when he was himself, they are worth everything else he ever did."

In such words was Milne's own personality revealed. The pursuit of worldly possessions meant nothing to him ; what he wanted was time, plenty of time to himself, to muse upon the pattern of the forest outside his door or upon arrangements of bowls and bunches of wild flowers in his hut— time, too, for painting them again and again in compositions set down lightly and quickly, with compression of feeling and economy of means. So, partly in order to save money and partly to have all the days and hours he wanted for painting, he had taken to the woods to live, first on the shores of Lake Temagami in northern Ontario, then, after a brief period in a farming village, in this one-room cabin in a remote corner of Muskoka, a few miles from Georgian Bay, where he dwelt from 1932 to 1939.

" Since art is æsthetic emotion, exhausting, to be sustained intensely for only a short time, the more quickly readable a picture is the greater its power," he once wrote.

Over the years he has sought to perfect a technique which would give these results. The method he achieved was based partly on a broken impressionist line, useful in illustration, which he picked up at an early stage, before

33. A. J. CASSON, R.C.A. (1898-   )
" Church at Magnetawan "

Oil: 37" × 45".   *National Gallery of Canada, Ottawa*

34. EDWIN H. HOLGATE, R.C.A. (1892-   )
" Ludovine "
Oil: 29½″ × 24¼″.   The Right Hon. Vincent Massey, C.H., Port Hope, Ontario

35.   LIONEL LeMOINE FitzGERALD (1890-   )
"Williamson's Garage"

Oil: 22″ × 18″.   National Gallery of Canada, Ottawa

36. PRUDENCE HEWARD (1896-1947)
" A Summer Day "
Oil: 24¾″ × 20¼″.   *John Fry, Esq., Cornwall, Ontario*

37. PARASKEVA CLARK (1898-   )
" Self-portrait "
Oil: 32¾" × 27". National Gallery of Canada, Ottawa

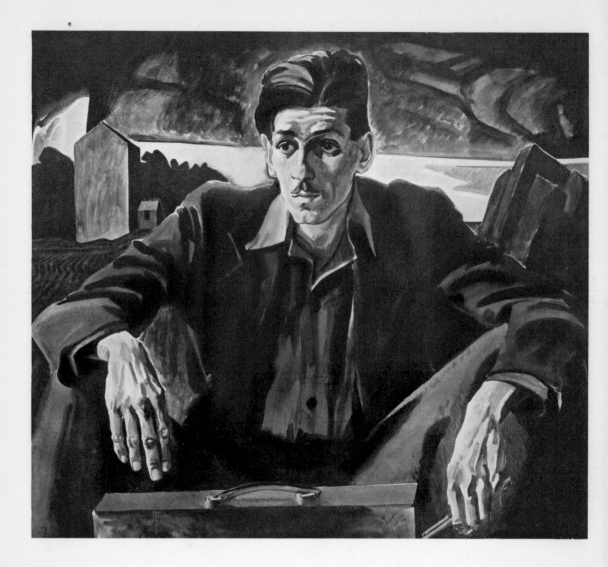

38. CHARLES COMFORT, R.C.A. (1900-   )
" Young Canadian "
Water-colour: 35¾″ × 41½″.   Hart House, University of Toronto

39. CARL SCHAEFER (1903-   )
"Stooks on John Voelzing's Farm"
Water-colour: 15½" × 22⅝". Ferargil Galleries, New York

40. W. A. OGILVIE (1901-   )
" Bombed Houses, Caen, Normandy "
Oil: 30″ × 24″. Canadian War Collection, National Gallery of Canada, Ottawa

1910, about the time he finished his studies in New York. Taken by itself, this method was superficial enough, but developed and elaborated as it was by Milne, it soon became something both intimate and at the same time compelling in the very briefness of its visual references. This can be seen from the water-colour, *The Mountains, 1917* (Plate 41), which was done in 1920 in the Adirondacks.

In his most characteristic work, he tends to note the actual scene before him in a few sensitive lines of drawing, then he adds an almost mathematical balance of large areas of white and of black or other dark values, and finally he enlivens the composition with many small and delicate touches of local colour. The colours he uses, however, are rarely linked directly to Nature ; he employs them more often for decorative than for realistic effects. This cool and intellectual approach of his is the product of long years of thought and reflection, of years of solitude devoted to the study of his craft.

David Milne was born on a farm in Bruce County, Ontario. His early life had a conspicuously rural setting, even to the few years he spent as a country school teacher. But, as a child and as a young man, he always liked to draw. So, having saved enough money from teaching, he went in 1904 to New York to study painting, where he joined the Art Students League. So quickly did his talents develop that by 1913 his work was considered interesting enough to be exhibited at the famous Armory show of that year in New York, in which modern painting from both Europe and America was first introduced to the public of this continent. Metropolitan life, however, did not attract him. He sought a less hurried pace of existence. This he found by moving to a small village called Boston Corners in a secluded part of New York state. Then, about 1918, he was offered a post as a Canadian war artist, and from this assignment he brought back a large collection of water-colours which are now in the War Memorials Collection in Ottawa.

Despite such official recognition, he remained for some time little known in Canada, and when he returned permanently to his native province in 1928, his work met at first with an almost total lack of understanding, on the part of both the public and collectors. Happily, in 1935, Vincent Massey, much attracted by some canvases by Milne which he had seen in an exhibition, offered to become his patron, and, Milne having agreed, Massey bought enough of his paintings to free the artist from immediate financial worries, and he also helped to ensure that Milne's work was in future more widely displayed.

Ten years ago, visiting a retrospective exhibition of his paintings, I wrote : " Milne, although he never went to Paris to study and has always been content with his little villages in upper New York state or in rural Ontario, has produced, through a mere attempt to be himself, delicate, sweetly logical landscapes of barns and wide-porched farmhouses, still lifes of jam jars and sugar bags on kitchen tables, which remind one neither of square dances nor of cross-road general stores, but rather of the bitter tang, the quick dry vitality, of French vermouth."

Seeing at the same time the canvas, *Water-lilies, Temagami* (Plate 42), which is now in the collection of Hart House, Toronto, I added : " Here one notices the quick, blunted contours of his drawing, the neat dry colours and patches of white without any colour, blank areas that set the eye to hovering lightly over the hues of violet or blue at the edges of flowers or bowl or window ledge. I should never have thought that such water-lilies, as modern in spirit as an interior of light steel and fabric furniture in the rooms of one of those new flats off the Bois de Boulogne in Paris, could have been painted by a man in an old blue jacket and ski-ing pants. But I have seen him now in a hut in the woods, have slept on patches of dried moss brought in from the edges of the swamp, and he has told me of another cabin on the shores of Lake Temagami, where he painted water-lilies all one summer in 1929. So I know better now and I know that the mind can distil as delicate a pattern from the leaves and trunks of the raw forest or from a deal table with a wash basin and a pot of geraniums as from the pleached and faded trees of the Royal Gardens at Versailles."

In 1938 he left Muskoka, and since then he has been living in Toronto and in one or two smaller towns in Ontario. To-day his work has become more varied in its reference. Painting urban streets, he finds in them a greater tensity of mood, which he expresses in darker tones in his oils, or in his water-colours with more strongly brushed-in washes and fewer of those open white areas which were once so typical of his style. Also a delicious quality of fantasy can now sometimes be detected. For a few years he deliberately emphasised such qualities of the imagination in a series of paintings, which ranged from snowflakes falling over Byzantine churches— *Snow over Bethlehem*[1] he called one of these—to conversation pieces involving Kings and Queens and Knaves who seemed to have stepped directly from a pack of playing cards. He also did several water-colours on the theme of St. Francis and the animals. In the one reproduced as Plate X the saint is followed by elephants and tigers, but there is a patch of Ontario forest in the background, and from it a few obviously Canadian animals look out in wonderment upon the procession.

Most of these fantasies are not the deceptively naïve and spontaneous creations which they appear to be at first glance. To gain their basic simplicity of statement he has done many of them, after a first tentative beginning, over and over again, until he has become sure that a certain compactness of vision has been achieved as well as the shock of the unusual in subject and treatment. As he himself has written, " The thing that makes a picture is the thing that makes dynamite—compression. It isn't a fire in the grass ; it is an explosion. Everything must hit at once."

[1] The water-colour is in the collection of the Art Gallery of Toronto.

PEGI NICOL MacLEOD (1904-1949)

Humanity on a Crowded Canvas

PEGI NICOL MacLEOD once wrote that to have one scene before her all day, whether it was her young daughter playing in the apartment, or the view of the bustling New York street beneath her windows, was to have it make such a tremendous impact upon her sensibilities that she had to paint it " or bust." She added, " To have it around all day removes perspective and I have kaleidoscope vision, but I must face it at last ! " So housework had to be dropped, to " let myself go (thick paint and wild abandon) . . ."

Her exuberant personality dominated everything she did, from the work she put into trying to promote exhibitions of Canadian art in New York to the efforts she made when in New Brunswick to improve standards of hand-craft design. Yet pervading all these interests was the great steady passion of her life, her painting. It became almost a painful and physical frustration to her if a day went by when illness, housework or visitors prevented her from doing at least one water-colour or oil sketch.

Her career as an artist was a varied one. It had its early roots deep in Canadian traditions. She could write of the paintings of Tom Thomson and J. E. H. MacDonald, " I have grown up with this art," and add, " it means so much to us as to be part of our living spirit."

After studying under Franklin Brownell in Ottawa and at the Ecole des Beaux-Arts in Montreal, she began in the late nineteen-twenties to do a few portrait studies and some strongly depicted scenes of the hills and rivers north of Ottawa, one of the finest examples of which is *The Log Run*, which won first prize for painting in the Willingdon Arts Competition in 1931.

About 1932-3, she, however, turned towards a more expressionist description of city scenes and communal activities. Best, from this period, are her many sketches and paintings of children digging in the public school gardens across the street from her parents' home in Ottawa. In these pictures, by the inter-relation of overlapping forms, by the mingling of sweeping lines of figures with the rhythmic contours of garden plots, she was able to convey, in purely visual terms, the emotional impact and excitement of group activity.

This tendency became more evident in her later paintings of crowded street scenes, done first when she went in 1934 to work in Toronto and then afterwards when she lived in New York. But, there in New York, the actions and events she watched were so multitudinous, the sensations she obtained from colour and motion so fluid and changing, that her own extreme sensitivity to all these stimuli proved at times to be almost her own undoing. She tried to put down on canvas and paper every aspect of the chaotic bustle that met her eyes from her windows on Eighty-Eighth Street ; she wished to leave nothing out. As a result, in many of those pictures the surface overflows with figures in motion, it is packed with now sinuous and graceful, now wavering and erratic, lines and shapes. Some of her conceptions seemed to demand the vast space of murals. Yet, remarkably enough, one sometimes comes across single water-colours—for instance, the impression she did of jostling crowds before the giant Christmas tree in Rockefeller Plaza—which in a small space manage, through subtle and brilliant colours and flowing line, to give adequately to the spectator all she wanted to express of humanity, in its variety, rising vigorous and triumphant over the mechanism of the metropolis.

From these struggles and experiments in New York, she garnered that experience of painting people in the mass, which served her in such good stead when, during the war, on the invitation of the National Gallery of Canada, she did in Ottawa a series of pictorial records of the Women's Services. She portrayed these uniformed girls at work, in barracks, at rest or on parade, in water-colours and oils which are strongly reminiscent of the highly charged atmosphere of those war days. Describing the records she was asked to make of these women in uniform, she wrote : " Yet the pictures painted of them to-day are for their daughters also. . . . Being documents, being history, they should be done in terms that will be understood by their children."

There was one æsthetic conviction in particular which always guided her in her work. It was, as she stated, that once a line was put down it possessed an expressive reality in itself, and should never be changed. So she voiced her conviction to her friends, Marian Scott and Lillian Freiman, when they were students together at the Ecole des Beaux-Arts in Montreal, and this conviction she retained as she grew to maturity. This was part and parcel of that quality of spontaneity which was most typical to her, both as a human being and as a painter.

The medium most natural for the exercise of her talents was water-colour, and in this she worked with great speed and concentration. Taking some favoured subject, such as the school gardens in Ottawa, she would, within a few weeks, make dozens of studies and as many finished compositions on this one theme. Later she would go on to do oil sketches of the same scene on wooden panels, and finally larger oil compositions on canvas.

She did not stop much to contemplate and construct. She rather rushed in with all her energy to do what her vision instinctively prompted. Yet as she kept doing over and over again the same subject, these compositions, often at first loosely organised, would tend, as she worked on new variations, to become more unified and coherent in their elements. In this way she did in New York some time in the year preceding her death a series of gouache and water-colour studies of pigeons on rooftops, which grew progressively more sure and rewarding in lyrically composed patterns of shapes and colours as the subject came to possess and control her imagination.

Even in those years when she was weighed down with the cares of house-work and of the bringing up of a young child, she kept on painting daily. Not only that, but she was experimenting constantly with new media, new approaches. Although one can find elements here and there in her work which tend to bring to mind many of the great modern masters, one would be wrong in seeking to imply any such direct derivations. Any notes of similarity to some of the contemporary expressionist masters were not obtained through imitation, but rather by the action of a daring young mind which instinctively sought to adjust itself in painting to the spirit of the times.

She conducted for many years the Observatory Summer School at the University of New Brunswick. Her influence as a teacher there was great, and her enthusiasm for promoting every aspect of Canadian art found wide-spread outlet in that province. At one period she did murals for the Wood-stock High School, and then later she created some gentle but ingenious designs for the making of hooked rugs by Maritime farm women, some of which designs have since been put into practical application. One of her friends has written that her coming each year to Fredericton appeared to be a most important happening in her life. "Her little group of students, the life up the hill, the visits to the open-air market, to the Experimental Farm, the fresh colouring of the fields, all fascinated her and lured her back each year. In 1948, when Fredericton was celebrating its centennial, she worked slavishly till early morning painting scenes for a university float—a tremendous bit of work. . . . She gave so freely. . . ."

Her long, intensely lived years in New York merely served to heighten her love for Canada, and she talked, before her untimely death in 1949, of the possibility of spending some extended period, even a complete year, in Fredericton or some other Canadian city, where she thought her culminating experiments might naturally unfold in a great blossoming of creative work. She was only forty-five years of age when she died, and the complete resolution of all her talents and experiments still lay before her.

LILLIAN FREIMAN (1908-   )

The Sensitive Vision

WHEN she turned from depicting Canadian landscape to portray instead crowded city streets and children in school gardens, Pegi Nicol MacLeod was following the same urge to paint humanity which had always been dominant in the work of Lillian Freiman, her friend of art school days.

Living with her family in one of the closely-built-up quarters of Montreal, Lillian Freiman early became accustomed to the congestion of urban life, and from the first found in it plenty of subjects to interest her. Although required at art school to do the usual quota of landscape sketches, her real passion from the very beginning was to draw people, alone or at work or play. Always nervous and sensitive, a harsh word from one of her teachers at the Beaux-Arts would send her into tears. Yet she would go without any sense of shyness down to the noisy, busy docks of the port, with her other close friend, Marian Scott, to paint carters and stevedores at work, loading or unloading the great freighters.

With the help of well-to-do relatives in Ottawa, she was able to leave Montreal in 1925 for France. By then she had had enough of schools and studios. Her resolve was to get what she could out of Paris by herself. So she frequented the museums, where she found how congenial to her own vision were the paintings of Degas and Toulouse-Lautrec, and, when she wanted to sketch from life, she went to the markets, above all to the bird market, for her subjects. Working among the crowds there, she would use a small pad of paper, and, keeping half-hidden so as not to let those about her know they were being recorded, she would make minute and rapid notes. From these she later composed her studio canvases, one of which, *The Bird Market*, is reproduced as Plate XI.

The intensely felt lines of her drawing, now broken, now sinuous, were at first no more than an expression of the joy she had found in depicting the scenes about her, but gradually as she matured she saw further, and through the nervous contours of her crayon and brush she began to underline, in addition, qualities of both mood and character in the faces she portrayed. She loved in particular to draw the children in the family with whom she boarded in Paris and also their young friends in the neighbourhood.

Her art alone mattered to her. In Montreal there had been so many other things which had had to come first, and it had never been simple for her to stand up to those who had thought she was wasting her time. But in

Paris, this reserved and introspective young girl, who was concerned only with art for its own sake, could feel accepted and at home. Also, if one craved to be solitary in the midst of people, then that, too, was possible. She was supremely contented there.

Following her own instinctive tastes, she found what she wanted from the arts of France, without bothering to participate much either in the life of the students or in their discussions of modern painting. But now that she has been so long away from France, she has begun to wonder, so she says, if she did not in those days remain too aloof from such debates—if perhaps she did not miss something by not becoming aware earlier of the power and significance of Rouault, whose work to-day begins to compel her attention more and more.

As with so many other young Canadian artists abroad, the threat of war in 1938 forced her to return to Canada. She lived for a year or so in Toronto, but she claims she could not adjust herself to the sober atmosphere of that city or to its self-conscious artistic life. Utterly discontented there, she painted little. Finally, in desperation, she decided to visit New York, and that visit has now turned into a sojourn of ten years. But a sojourn only it continues to be, for her dreams are still of Paris.

In the meantime, her work becomes better known generally through the interest taken in it by collectors and critics in New York. For instance, Dr. Julius S. Held, writing of it recently, said : " The harmonies which she creates have the mellow and nostalgic sweetness of a tune remembered from childhood. Her forms are sometimes well-defined and sometimes amorphous, and hence seem to create an existence which is neither fully concrete nor wholly ethereal. What holds them together is the same purity of lyrical feeling, so manifest in her graceful, linear rhythms and her iridescent colours. Her drawing occasionally has the masterly economy and grandeur of a renaissance artist."

While the tense atmosphere of Manhattan might not be expected to be conducive to her best work, she has, nevertheless, discovered in the neighbourhood of her studio on Eighth Avenue subjects in which she finds that same quiet delight she used to obtain from the scenes she sketched in Paris. For example, she has made friends in a nearby tenement with a Chinese family, whose members still retain their oriental traditions. Talking with them, playing with their children, she slyly sketches them as they eat or work without allowing them to be conscious that she is depicting their faces, for they have a strange and superstitious fear of being drawn. Afterwards, in her studio, she works on larger compositions based on these sketches. The best ones are of the round-faced and wide-eyed children and of their pets, two sleek and sleepy cats.

As her drawing has become more subtle and complicated in its elements, so also have the materials and techniques she uses. Working with mixtures of crayon and inks, of both opaque and transparent washes, with pencil, too, and sometimes charcoal, she gains from various combinations of these media her most satisfying effects. She also does smaller ink and wash drawings, the best of which are of circus scenes or of a gypsy band. This vagabond orchestra, which plays from time to time on nearby street corners, delights her in particular, and she is anxious to create some large and more elaborate compositions based on her sketches of these players. Much of her work is spontaneous, in the fashion that Pegi Nicol MacLeod's was, but she differs here in that she is willing to ponder and meditate at more length in her studio over the canvases she is working on, until slowly and eventually they emerge finished to her satisfaction.

Most of her New York friends are to be found either among her poorer neighbours or among musicians. That great musical centre, Carnegie Hall, has become her favourite haunt in recent years. There, every week or so, when important rehearsals are being held, she will sit quietly in the partially darkened auditorium and work with great speed on large lyrically conceived sketches of violinists, of famous conductors, or of singers, like Marian Anderson. These quickly and sensitively executed compositions of hers, with their combination of grace in drawing and realism of atmosphere, are reminiscent of Degas's pastels of ballet dancers or of Toulouse-Lautrec's studies of stage and opera and cabaret performers, but they possess at the same time a nervousness of her own and a modernity of mood.

In her studio, helping to keep alive her memories of Paris, are birdcages, hanging from the ceiling—a score or more of them of enamelled metal or lacquered wood, in gay colours and odd shapes. Beneath them, piled up in great stacks, is her work, amassed over many years. Although there is a demand for her paintings from discriminating collectors—a few years ago one of the most prominent dealers in New York held a show of her paintings which was most successful from the point of view of sales—she is always loath to part with her creations. Pegi Nicol MacLeod, in a letter, once related how she had come upon Lillian weeping in a corner of the hall where the dealer was exhibiting her pictures. The reason for her tears, she finally explained, was that most of the paintings had been sold !

41. DAVID MILNE (1882-   )
"The Mountains, 1917"

Water-colour: 15¼" × 22".   *National Gallery of Canada, Ottawa*

42. DAVID MILNE (1882-   )
"Water-lilies, Temagami"
Oil: 19½″ × 23½″. *Hart House, University of Toronto*

43. DAVID MILNE (1882-   )
"The Tower"
Water-colour: $14\frac{1}{4}'' \times 21\frac{1}{8}''$

44. LILLIAN FREIMAN (1908-   )
"Street Song"
Oil. 25 " × 31 ".

45. PEGI NICOL MacLEOD (1904-1949)
" School in a Garden "
Oil. Private Collection

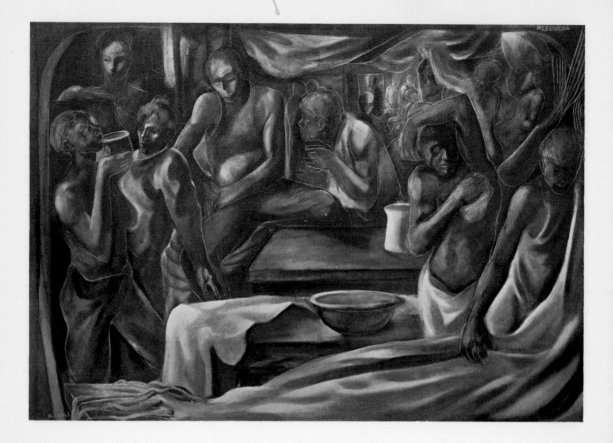

46. JACK NICHOLS (1921-   )
" Mess Deck "
Oil: 34" × 50". Canadian War Collection, National Gallery of Canada, Ottawa

47. B. C. BINNING (1909-   )
" Ships in Classical Calm "
Oil: 32″ × 40½″. National Gallery of Canada, Ottawa

48. FRITZ BRANDTNER (1896-   )
" City from a Night Train "
Oil: 41″ × 39⅜″

FRITZ BRANDTNER (1896-   )

Versatility in Design

EVERY aspect of design interests Fritz Brandtner. He paints oils and water-colours, ranging from boldly coloured landscapes and fantasies involving horses and riders to semi-abstractions of city streets, and, more recently, he has gone on to do some completely non-objective compositions. He has also completed a number of murals, including some carved in linoleum.

Until 1928 he lived and worked in what was, before Hitler's dark days of power, the Free City of Danzig. He had been born and educated there, but, as his father was an Austrian, he escaped most of the rigidities of the local Prussian conceptions of upbringing and discipline. Conscripted during the war of 1914-18 into the German Army, he was captured by the Allies and spent some time in prison camps. There he took up sketching as a hobby, and when peace came he felt competent enough, upon returning home, to set himself up as a commercial artist. Soon he was receiving enough commissions to make a moderate living. Later he took time off to study painting at the University of Danzig. But his joys in the cultural activities which the city provided, and in the healthy recreations it afforded, such as swimming in the Baltic or riding horses bareback with boisterous companions in swift races along the flat, sandy beaches close by, were quickly dissipated by the riots which came to mark the life of the Free City as the revolutionary agitations of the Nazis spread outwards from the Reich. Brandtner was a firm democrat, also a convinced internationalist, and he sensed quickly enough how serious was the menace of the future. He decided to turn his back on his past and to emigrate to Canada, a nation he knew to be a firm democracy ; although otherwise it was a land utterly strange to him, except for the totem poles and other Indian art he had seen in museums.

Arriving in Winnipeg in 1928, he had to take odd jobs at first ; in fact, for about a year he was a house painter. Then, as he painfully adjusted himself to his new surroundings, he was able to find a fairly good position in the studio of an engraving plant. In his spare time he began to sketch the tumble-down houses on the back streets of this western city or the busy railway yards and the adjoining riverside with its warehouses and steel bridges ; he also did some more intimate studies of workers on street corners and of charwomen scrubbing floors.

After he had settled in Montreal in 1934, his work gradually began to take on a more abstract character. To build up shapes by means of constructional arrangements of line is the aim of most of his drawing and painting to-day. This even applies to the work he did one summer recently in Georgian Bay, where he went, in a searching mood, to find out how he, the German emigrant, newly become a Canadian citizen, would react to those famed northern landscapes of lake and rock and pine which had so inspired the members of the Group of Seven. He reacted by painting them in non-naturalistic colours which, while they may shock the more doggedly faithful followers of Jackson and MacDonald, nevertheless often do convey the dark and sometimes forbidding strength of those rock-bound scenes.

Whereas in Germany his colours had tended to be fairly subdued, they have now become more vivid, strongly personal and almost arbitrary in choice. He also, on occasion, goes in for an almost metallic brightness in his oils, as can be seen in most of those he did of Georgian Bay.

His most interesting experiments of late have been concerned with a kind of constructivist art. Cutting out interlocking strips of coloured cardboard, he builds them up into involved three-dimensional forms. These, being accordion-like, can be pulled apart or pressed together to create amazing variations of shapes. Yet throughout all the variations there runs a constant cohesion of design which it is outside the will of the artist to change, for it is dictated by the involved geometry of the object itself, by the mechanics of stress and strain of its related parts. He has now painted a series of " still lifes " describing a few of these variations in structure. The resulting compositions, when hung on the wall side by side, are seen to have the same closely woven thread of relationship running throughout as we associate in music with the counterpoint of a fugue.

From these studies in the higher realms of form, Brandtner obtains that sureness of design so evident in the best of his larger and more recent paintings. Such a one is *City from a Night Train* (Plate 48). Along with the intense degree of abstraction which this composition possesses, Brandtner has managed to convey at the same time a hint of that fleeting mystery which always cloaks even the most commonplace quarters of a great city when viewed at night from the window of a passing express.

In Canada, the first major recognition he received came in 1933 when he was commissioned by the Saskatchewan Government to prepare a 320-foot mural for the World's Wheat Fair in Regina. Later, in Montreal, he began to receive other more varied commissions ; for example, in that city he has done etched glass panels for the Bell Telephone building, carved stone plaques for the new Canadian National Railways station, and a linoleum panel, incised and enamelled in gay colours, for the Berkeley Hotel.

He has been particularly anxious to promote the use of linoleum as a medium for mural decoration, and he has produced other panels of this kind, both large and small. Writing of his aims and technique in this medium, he states :

XI. LILLIAN FREIMAN (1908-   )
"Bird Market"
Oil: 24½″ × 22½″. *H. O. McCurry, Esq., Ottawa*

"Only when there is a clear relationship between material, design, technique and texture do we feel that the result we have achieved in our work is dynamic. The material has to have a chance to take part in shaping the idea. Linoleum is a synthetic material, it is man-made in contrast to wood, which is an organic substance. As such, linoleum calls up ideas that lead us away from pure representation and towards the abstract. Therefore abstract qualities of design will give the greatest satisfaction, will bring an intense life of their own into linoleum carvings. . . . The combining of carved and painted surfaces, in such dimensions as those offered us by complete walls, will create new sensations of æsthetic enjoyment for the community as a whole, and give the artist new and unexpected opportunities for expressing his ideas about the world surrounding him."

But despite his most genuine talent in this direction, he rarely finds an architect or contractor who is willing to adopt anything but the most naturalistic type of a decoration for a building, a restaurant or an office, and so his urge to work out new designs in linoleum has been languishing of late. The same applies to patterns he does for textiles and to his posters and book jackets. He is constantly working up designs of that nature in his studio but he manages to sell few of them. As far as the application of art to industry is concerned, he is ahead of his time in Canada.

B. C. BINNING (1909-   )

A New Architecture in Paint

TOO many Canadian artists, once they have obtained a certain facility of execution or have found some novel mode of expression, proceed to stick too long with it. Having exhausted the ore they are digging, they find themselves stranded with no new riches to mine and nothing to work on save the slagheaps of the past, which now lie piled up about them. It is good, then, to find a Vancouver artist, B. C. Binning, first shocking, then stimulating his admirers by the sudden and complete change he has made during the past several years in both his style and achievements.

Born on the Canadian prairies, Binning at an early age moved with his family to Vancouver to live. There he developed a love of small boats, of sail and tackle, and he used to make frequent trips on afternoons and holidays to the nearby bays and inlets with their sandy beaches and rocky headlands and giant overhanging spruce and fir forests. As he grew up he studied art, both in London and New York ; later, following his return home, he obtained the post of instructor of drawing at the Vancouver School of Art.

From then on, his principal delight was to sketch in his spare time all the varied activities of the waterfront. A tall man of fine appearance, possessed of a pleasant and almost expansive personality, his presence was accepted without question by both boatmen and holidaymakers, and also by that shifting group of poorer workers who live on the jerry-built houseboats and rafts which line the smaller coves and the outer shores of Vancouver's harbour and inlet. He put them into his drawings along with the boats. Sometimes he drew people alone, but even then, when the subject was a man seated in sober meditation, or a young girl reclining within a delicate tracery of foliage, you would almost invariably find in the background, beyond a distant strip of beach, the brief outline of a sail or of some receding row-boat. These row-boats, large or small, in multitudes and alone, or half-hidden beneath fringes of trees and underbrush, became the personal signature to all his work.

By 1947 Binning had achieved a widespread reputation for the excellence of his drawings, which by then had been shown in various exhibitions and written about at length in reviews and articles. Some critics had mentioned their " psychological connotations," also the surface vitality given them by the repetitions of certain forms such as " flags, anchors, oars, driftwood and wiggling ropes." Others had noted " how his line wanders with a delicate waywardness," or, conversely, had remarked upon " his concern for surface

76

organisation, a tendency to work up and over the picture plane in the manner of a Persian tapestry." But however they reacted to his work, all critics were united in stressing that he, alone among Canadian artists, was putting the full concentration of his expression into pen-and-ink drawing.

Everyone was astonished when in 1949 he began to show not only an interest in oil painting but also an ability to demonstrate in this medium the possibilities of a new architecture in paint. Gone were the wayward lines ; all was now emphasis on surface textures in pigment and on abstraction of form.

However, he did not give up his old and constant love of row-boats, sailing sloops and dinghies. These, in a moving and changing panorama over the water, he still watches daily, as he looks down upon that great and spreading bay which lies beneath the steeply wooded slopes upon which he has built his home in West Vancouver. But it is the larger craft, the coastal vessels, passing down the bay on their way to the various ports of the mountainous coast of British Columbia, or the liners and freighters, steaming seawards to the Pacific and the Orient, which provide the imposing shapes and dimensions most suitable to his new interpretations. The paintings he does now of ships are highly formalised ; in the hulls and riggings, which he draws, he creates a cool and almost mathematical balance between subtle curves and precise straight lines.

In 1948 he was given a sabbatical year from his teaching duties at the Vancouver School of Art. This was when he decided to effect the transition from drawing to painting.

" It was," he writes, " a year of revaluation and experiment, brooding, despair and in the end a small ray of hope : ten large canvases and a few small ones." He adds : " In looking at myself I saw with a certain amount of justification (because both my grandfathers were architects) a strong feeling towards those qualities known as ' architectural ' in painting. This quality may have accentuated itself, just then, because I was also designing and supervising the building of two houses.[1] Whatever the reason, I began to feel greatly both the discipline of Architecture and its formal ideas, things like : the flat of the picture plane, the strong boundaries of the frame, the simple strength of the truly architectural form and its relating space, the contrasting play of line, the force of colour when freed from atmosphere and effect. Or perhaps it was the sudden realisation of what can happen creatively when one frees not only colour, but form and everything else, from visual accident and recreates through the formal and architectural approach. Whatever it was, it hit me like a ton of very architectural bricks."

" Forms and Ideas," he goes on to explain, " must fuse," and his problem here has been to fuse the lyric idea, which was so present in the best of his

[1] He had previously built one for himself which had attracted nation-wide attention for its refined use of British Columbia fir and cedar for all exterior and interior construction.

earlier drawings, with these new architectural values. In his own way, he wanted to do what Seurat had done before him by other methods. In many ways, *Ships in Classical Calm* (Plate 47) is one of the best of his new paintings. Interesting also is *The White Ship*, in which, despite its abstraction of forms, there remains a hint of his former " delicate waywardness " in drawing.

" You may ask now," he notes, " why ships ? Being a seaside person, small boats, ships and things of the sea are old loves of mine—I know them well and I find them ready forms for interpretation. They can be lyric, no doubt about that, grand and elegant with dignity and power, or jolly and happy for joy. They abstract well. . . ."

In *Small Boats Frolicking near a Blue Diving Tower*, now in the collection of Hart House in Toronto, he has retained some of that spirit of relaxation and humour which was implicit in the finest of his earlier drawings. In this painting, done in 1949, he has gone back to the gentler aspect of the sheltered coves and away from the great, more dramatic ships of his first architectural arrangements. The background areas are blue and yellow greys, with noticeable qualities of texture in the pigment, while the triangles of the ships and flags are white or black or bright blues and reds.

" For me, at least," he explains, " it has some of that lovely feeling I get when I see boats bobbing and rolling to each other at anchor on a bright summer day with the sea running, and that is a joyous experience."

It is " this business of serious joy " that Binning thinks is neglected too much in Canadian painting. A fine expression of joy, in his opinion, can be and should be as significant a basis for serious art as are any of the sterner moods of life.

As for the suggestion that he has now dropped his interest in pure drawing to devote himself entirely to doing oils on canvas, he replies : " Have I given up drawing ? Good lord, no ! The wonder of a line is eternal ! " But here he makes a distinction as to purpose. " In my drawing," he states, " the medium is used as a commentary on what I see, whereas in painting it is an interpretation of what I feel."

Binning, who now teaches fine arts at the University of British Columbia, believes that in his recent painting he is getting at the essential by abstraction, whereas before he " played too much with the incidental, accidental and anecdotal." " Of future directions," he concludes, " one can only dream, and I dream of great, quiet spatial ideas and rich colour and the sea and the coast."

XII. GOODRIDGE ROBERTS (1904-   )
"Nude"
Oil: $39\frac{1}{4}'' \times 21\frac{5}{8}''$. *National Gallery of Canada, Ottawa*

JACK NICHOLS (1921-   )

The Tension Beneath Appearances

JACK NICHOLS was born in 1921, so he is of that youngest generation of Canadian artists who were brought up in the depression and who were still in their adolescence when war broke out in 1939. Yet, while his career has in a sense only just begun, he has already a remarkable record of achievement behind him. Commissioned in 1943 to do paintings for the Canadian merchant marine, he was made in the following year an official Navy war artist. Then, back from overseas only a short time, he was awarded a Guggenheim Fellowship, enabling him to spend a year doing advanced creative work in the United States, which year he devoted partly to painting but mainly to the study of lithography. Since then he has taught at the Vancouver School of Art, and he is now living and working in his own studio in Toronto.

As a background to these successes are the struggles of his earlier youth. Both his parents died while he was still a child in Montreal, and at fourteen he was obliged to take whatever job he could in order to earn his bread and board.

" Even then," as Andrew Bell has said in a tribute he recently paid Nichols in the columns of *Canadian Art*, " he was convinced that he could and would be an artist, and thereafter that conviction, that determination, set the pattern of his life. Any job would do—dishwasher, waiter, deckhand. Once he had a slender margin of resources he would quit the job, whatever it might be, and paint. When the money was exhausted he started all over again.

" Clearly, in these circumstances, there was no chance for a formal art education, and he never had one. . . . Still, in different ways, and at different times," as Bell adds, " three men, Louis Muhlstock, F. H. Varley, and Douglas Duncan, all aided and encouraged him."

His friend, Muhlstock, who had also grown up in the poorer quarters of Montreal, gave him his first guidance in figure drawing, and, for practice in sketching, he introduced him to that " poor man's studio," the Turkish baths of the neighbourhood, where the proprietor allowed them both to come and sketch, whenever they wanted, in the vaporous atmosphere of the steam and shower rooms. There were also the few months he spent in Ottawa in 1938, taking some tuition from Varley, and then his meeting later with Douglas Duncan of the Picture Loan Society in Toronto. Duncan, besides selling quite a few of his paintings for him, was also generous in the personal appreciation and informed criticism he gave Nichols in the work he was

79

doing. In this way, the young artist obtained that increased confidence which enabled him to continue painting, despite those intervals of relative poverty into which he was sometimes plunged.

" In recent years the work of Nichols," to quote again from the article by Bell, " has appeared in a wide variety of exhibitions. The subjects have always been people, usually in groups, doing things habitual to their daily lives. They have been people, too, whose emotions and activities were a part of the artist's own experience. Thus, in the pre-1943 period, it was workmen playing pool, coloured folk dancing in a small, smoky hall, knots of emaciated children, the bitter urban fruit of the depression of the thirties."

A combination of state patronage and the war gave him his first chance to devote his full time to art. His *Rescue at Sea* won the first prize for the best picture in the exhibition of the Canadian Group of Painters in 1945, and when a comprehensive showing of official war art was held in Ottawa in 1946 it became obvious that Nichol's *Mess Deck Scene* (Plate 46), and even more particularly his *Normandy Scene, Beach in " Gold " Area*, had more of the monumental and less of the anecdotal than most of the other war contributions on view.

" This war work," according to Bell, " was an adaptation of his earlier experience and passionate interest in humanity to the circumstances of his new assignment. Now he was painting on a larger canvas, figuratively and literally. Yet the emphasis on the human form—and its emotional response to the life of which he was a part—was the same. (Nichols says he can't paint anything he doesn't intimately know. It was several months, for example, before he felt the ocean to be really in his system. . .)"

Describing the sketches in charcoal or crayon, and the larger works in pencil and thin oil, which he was doing previous to his departure for the United States in 1947, Bell explains : " In all there is a marked emphasis on broad form, a stern selectivity of detail, and slight colour range. With Nichols, drawing comes first, and it is in muted tones that so far he has felt best able to achieve harmony and unity in his subjects."

Nichols wants art to reach people in every available form. More time and energy he therefore thinks should be devoted by artists to the making and distribution of original prints in various media at moderate prices, so that everyone who wants to own a work of art can afford to buy one. For this reason, when he was in California on his Guggenheim Fellowship, he began to take an enthusiastic interest in lithography. At first the work he printed from the stone was groping and experimental ; this was because he was moving forward slowly into what was for him an entirely new technique. Later he was to obtain a more sensitive and, at the same time, brooding quality from the use of heavy, black tones. His best lithographs of that period depict the tired and worn but still vital faces of young mothers, sitting asleep or half-awake with their children in the crowded bus terminals of cities

49. JOHN LYMAN (1886-   )
" Still Life on Table "
Oil: 16″ × 20″. Dominion Gallery, Montreal

50. GOODRIDGE ROBERTS (1904-   )
"Portrait"
Oil: 34″ × 25″.   Mr. and Mrs. Gérald Rhéaume, Montreal

51. GOODRIDGE ROBERTS (1904-   )
" Still Life with Teapot and Coral Tablecloth "
Oil: 30″ × 38″. Dominion Gallery, Montreal

52. GOODRIDGE ROBERTS (1904-   )
" Landscape near Lake Orford "
Water-colour: 21¼″ × 29½″. *National Gallery of Canada, Ottawa*

53. JACK HUMPHREY (1901-   )
" Main Street, Afternoon "
Water-colour: 21" × 28½".   Dr. George Skinner, Saint John, New Brunswick

54. LOUIS MUHLSTOCK (1904-   )
" Street Corner, Montreal "
Oil: 36″ × 32⅜″. Mrs. Alison Palmer, Montreal

55. STANLEY COSGROVE (1911-   )
"Portrait of a Young Woman"

Oil: 26" × 20".   Musée de la Province de Québec, Quebec City

56. STANLEY COSGROVE (1911-   )
"Landscape"
Oil: 23¾" × 28¾".   Mrs. H. A. Dyde, Edmonton

57. ALFRED PELLAN (1906-   )
" Surprise Académique "
Oil: 82″ × 66″.   Maurice Corbeil, Esq., Montreal

58. ALFRED PELLAN (1906-   )
" Les Iles de la Nuit "

Water-colour and ink: 8″ × 7″.   Madame Marck Drouin, Quebec City

59. ALFRED PELLAN (1906-   )
"Symphonie"
Oil: 64" × 51". Maurice Corbeil, Esq., Montreal

60. PAUL-ÉMILE BORDUAS (1905-   )
"La Cavale Infernale"
Oil: 15¾" × 18½".   Luc Choquette, Esq., Montreal

61. PAUL-ÉMILE BORDUAS (1905-   )
" Composition "
Gouache: 19″ × 23″

62. PAUL-ÉMILE BORDUAS (1905-   )
" La Femme au Bijou "
Oil: 32″ × 43″

63. JACQUES DE TONNANCOUR (1917-   )
"Les Gants de Filet"
Oil: 36″ × 24¼″. Joseph Barcelo, Esq., Montreal

64. JACQUES DE TONNANCOUR (1917-   )
"Still Life with Round Table"
Oil: 32″ × 36″

such as Memphis and New Orleans, which he visited on his travels across the southern states. Looking at these more powerful prints of his, one wonders perhaps if the less vibrant disposition of black and white is not more congenial to his probing, contemplative nature than is the more sensual play of strong and rich pigments. But he wants also to be able to use colour at times and, now that he has settled down to what he hopes will be several unbroken years of creative activity in his studio in Toronto, he has decided to divide his time equally between lithography and certain more sustained experiments in formal construction in painting. In these he hopes to bring colour more expressively than before into his interpretations of human environment.

He wants especially to continue to depict, as best he may, the inner substance which determines the outward actions of people. For example, in one of the finest of his imaginative portraits, *Boy with Flute*, he has pressed his whole composition, including the subsidiary figures in the background, into the job of amplifying and explaining the emotional significance of the central character. His people—the people in his paintings—are composites. Nichols never uses models : his types are drawn from memories of all manner of persons he has made friends with and observed in the world he knows. As for his own attitude to humanity, he is willing to smile when there is true laughter of the spirit to be described, or he is willing to extend pity when he senses unhappiness behind the ironic or contradictory actions into which his fellow-men stumble. But he will never indulge in satire. He feels far too strongly and too personally the tensions of the modern community to believe that mordant wit can have any place in the true humour of the art he wishes to create.

As he puts it in his own words : " Understanding is never a question of just knowledge. It is also a problem of deep feeling."

JOHN LYMAN (1886-   )

Artist and Critic

"TRADITION does not come from rocks and trees," John Lyman once wrote, "it comes from the hearts and minds of men." Also in describing James Wilson Morrice, he said—and this comment in itself reveals as much as anything else can the essentials of his critical approach to art in Canada : "He was just a painter, which is perhaps not such a bad thing for a painter to be."

Lyman, who has so much influenced the newer generation of artists in Montreal by means of his essays and articles on æsthetics and by the profound and generous interest he has shown in the work of painters of such diverse talents as Roberts and Borduas, is no longer young. He was born in 1886, which makes him about the same age as A. Y. Jackson and Arthur Lismer. But, unlike those men, who during the nineteen-twenties so successfully spread the gospel of nationalism, Lyman has never at any time shown the slightest enthusiasm for regionalism in art. In fact, he has vigorously opposed all such tendencies. "The talk of the Canadian scene has gone sour," he wrote in 1948, and he added : "The real Canadian scene is in the consciousness of Canadian painters, whatever the object of their thought."

To understand the position of Lyman both as a critic and as a painter, one must first grasp how wide is his background of culture and travel, how natural his liberal cultivation of mind.

As a young man, after going to McGill University in Montreal and studying for a while to be an architect, he decided that he would like to be a painter instead. So he attended several art schools in France and England, including one conducted by Henri Matisse in Paris before the First Great War. When he first showed his work in Canada in 1913, it was considered too advanced by those who were then the arbiters of taste in Montreal. He was admonished by these pundits for "his atrocious disregard of every known canon of art," mainly because, one would gather, he simplified his drawing and did not stick closely enough to commonplace and naturalistic colours in the pigments he used. But he was no more a *fauve*, in the sense of insisting on painting in pure and undivided colours and exuberant line, than Morrice was.

Possessing a private income, Lyman was not forced, as some of the other younger painters of those days were, to modify his ideas in order to earn a living and be accepted into the limited artistic cliques which were dominant in Montreal during the first quarter of the century. Instead, he went back to Europe and stayed there for almost another twenty years, except for occasional visits home or to Bermuda and the West Indies. In 1931, as the economic depression began to deepen, he returned to Canada, and since that date he has been living almost continuously in Montreal.

As far as cultural values generally were concerned in Canada, the shock of the slump brought one salutary result. The younger generation of Canadians began to lose that preoccupation with material values which had so obsessed many of their elders during the previous few decades. The time was ripe for new ideas and new movements in Canadian painting. Lyman, fortified by his wide knowledge of contemporary artistic developments in France and equipped, as he was, with a sound understanding of æsthetic thought generally, was now able, through the many articles of criticism he wrote and the lectures he gave, to do much to bring about a better conception of what " living art " really was and could be in Canada.

Disinterested to the point of neglecting his own work in favour of encouraging the development of a freer, a more sensitive, a less pontifical growth of painting in Canada, Lyman now devoted a large part of his energies to the organisation of the Contemporary Arts Society. This Society, composed of sympathetic laymen and independent artists, was founded in 1939. The real coherence of its members lay in their conviction that the art of painting could never be considered as a mere technique adapted to other purposes, whether regional, social or didactic. The artists included Lyman, Borduas, Roberts, Brandtner, Muhlstock, Philip Surrey, Marian Scott and Louise Gadbois, all from Montreal, and Jack Humphrey from New Brunswick. While some of them inclined towards " representation " and others towards " non-representation," the tendency was away from any emphasis on description towards a more spontaneous poetry of form.

Too often artistic activities in Canada tend to be divided by race and language. But this Society managed to surmount such difficulties. Lyman, who was its first president, was completely bilingual, as were several other of its members. As a result, the Society formed a link between those two cultures, the Anglo-Saxon and the Gallic, which exist in Montreal. Its fusing of these two mentalities into a unified enthusiasm for living art was a great accomplishment. That this Society, after ten years of useful existence, should now have disbanded is unfortunate, but perhaps to be expected in view of the rapid growth of so many other diversified activities among painters in Montreal.

Lyman's great contribution to-day as before is in the role of mentor and critic. But one must not neglect the qualities which his best paintings undoubtedly possess. Compared with those of many of his colleagues they may seem to be in a minor key. Certainly they have nothing of the revolutionary impact which one associates with many types of modern art. In his work there is an even balance between sensibility and intellect, and one can agree with his friend, Dr. Paul Dumas, that most of his pictures present the "expression of a highly civilised personality through harmonious forms and serene, limpid colours." We might have reproduced here one of his landscapes or one of his figure studies, but instead we have chosen a small painting of the mildest of possible subjects, the quiet corner of an unpretentious sitting-room. This picture, *Still Life on Table* (Plate 49), in its simplicity displays most adequately the "discreet charm which emanates from his art," a charm which "recalls the effect of chamber music."

GOODRIDGE ROBERTS (1904-   )

A Grave Poetry in Paint

A QUALITY of sustained and sober reflection marks the work of Goodridge Roberts. Trees, human figures, flowers, hills—all these rest in equilibrium. The more romantic aspects of Nature do not appeal to him, nor is he concerned with the drama of character and emotion in the faces of the people he portrays. His business is rather painting itself, the interplay of colour and texture and form. Social content he leaves to the sociologists, the more personal emotions to the psychologists, and geographical detail to the illustrators.

" I like," he writes in describing his point of view, " to paint people sitting, standing or reclining, quite static, serene and impersonal. Up to now, anyway, I have avoided painting old or ugly people. I like to paint young people in the nude—ones who have as yet retained their grace with a quality of both the skeleton and the young flower about them, before they have filled out and settled down into solid citizens, or have become types, whether of success or failure."

While, to many of his admirers, his best work has been done in oils and figure painting, there are others who prefer his distinctly personal creations in water-colour, which usually depict scenes of bush and lake or of the semi-cultivated countryside in the Laurentian Hills or in the Eastern Townships of Quebec. They are built with a free brush, with what are usually deceptively simple colour schemes and with no resort whatsoever to melodramatic effects.

His water-colours, however, have emerged slowly from difficult beginnings. He had to fight his way, during the summers of 1932 and 1933, with many a ragged and crumpled sheet of paper to mark his failures, towards his first grasp of how to use this medium to convey what he wanted to express.

Strangely enough it was not desire, nor conversely was it any puritanical drive to submit himself to arduous tasks, which impelled him to paint in water-colour. It was rather temporary poverty, the poverty of a young man, who had to paint even if he couldn't always eat, and who, because he couldn't afford to buy oils or easels or canvas, was forced into using paper and washes instead. But having once turned to the task, he then put the whole force of his being into the job, and in the end he succeeded in forcing the medium to bend to his will.

From these struggles he has obtained his own peculiar power of rendering, not that facile grace or charm which is often associated with water-colour, but instead more solid virtues, such as a calm cohesion of fluid forms and a profundity of feeling.

Some of these compositions of Quebec scenery can best be described as organic abstractions based on natural forms. Others are of immobile trees and quiescent lakes, fixed in space, or as Jacques de Tonnancour has written of both his water-colours and oils, " his landscapes sleep in time."

Roberts is a Canadian from many generations back ; his family is a distinguished one in which literature and poetry have always taken root and flourished. His uncle, Sir Charles G. D. Roberts, was the author of numerous volumes of verse of varying mood, and Bliss Carman, that fine poet of Canadian nature, was also one of his relatives. Goodridge, or " Goody " as his friends call him, has, however, always been more interested in the plastic quality of paint than in the rhythm of words. After leaving high school, he immediately began to study art, and from Montreal went to New York, where he worked under John Sloan and Max Weber at the Art Students League. Coming back to Canada, he taught art in Ottawa for a while. But he was never really able to combine teaching with painting, so he decided in the summer of 1932 to give up his classes, and retaining only one pupil from whom he earned an income of a dollar or so a week—his sole revenue in those days—he moved into a tent on a hilltop near the Gatineau River and there he painted steadily for several months.

This was when he began to do his first water-colours. The location " on an elevation with a broad expanse of landscape below me—with a winding river and many clumps of trees, ploughed fields, and pastures—an expanse in which I can let my imagination wander and out of which I can organise my picture," was ideal for his purpose, and he returned to paint close by in 1933.

His first exhibition, held in Montreal in the autumn of that year, brought him into touch with John Lyman, who turned out to be most sympathetic and constructive in the criticism and encouragement he now gave Roberts. Lyman did much to reinforce the younger painter in his belief that an artist's obligation is not to record the appearance of things, but that his duty is rather towards himself, as Nature can only be expressed in paint through one's own sensibility and awareness and through the development of one's own personality.

Lyman wrote to Roberts at this time : " I like your work immensely for its terse characterisation in drawing and your rare ability to *see* colour, not merely to use it illustratively or as a schematic ornament."

During the next three years Roberts held a post as resident artist and art instructor at Queen's University in Kingston, Ontario. Once more he found himself unable both to paint and to teach at the same time. Nevertheless, he appears to have gained something from this fallow period, for as soon as he settled down in Montreal in 1936, he immediately entered upon a new stage of fresh and fruitful activity. His oils and his water-colours, both of landscapes and figures, now began to sell—although he later did have to do some teaching to supplement his income—and his work was soon being praised widely by most critics. Robert Ayre, for example, wrote of him in 1940 : " The intensity of his feeling for the hills is held in check by a fundamental sobriety. He is not lyric, he does not rhapsodise or senti-mentalise, but I do not think I should call him austere, since austere suggests severity ; he is calm."

The silent, solitary stubbornness of the man, as he goes about creating his images, is now and then revealed in the lack of grace in the surface of his oil painting, in the heavy, almost gauche, roughness with which his pigment is sometimes applied, particularly in a few of his still lifes of flowers and fruit. Yet his work is always moving forward, even if there are spells of what he calls " slurring over problems," periods which bother his conscience and make him say that he would like to change and try his hand at sculpture. He returns, nevertheless, steadfastly to his concentration upon painting. He has been experimenting with greater strength of colour in some of his still lifes ; also a year or so ago he attempted something entirely new, a series of large compositions in pastel ; and recently, in reference to the future, he wrote that he wanted to do some very large canvases of " groups of people acting out a contemporary play (as Giotto did)."

Given a guarantee of annual exhibitions and sales by a dealer, he manages to-day to live on the proceeds of his painting alone, a rare triumph in Canada for any artist and particularly for one of such integral independence as Roberts.

Reserved, self-effacing, vague in gesture and speech, he presents himself as an enigma to those who do not know him well. Carrying his tall, slow-moving body through the city streets with head bowed and mind concentrated on his own thoughts, he has been aptly described by one friend as " a sleep-walker from birth." But this is the outer man, and if he appears to dream, these are not futile fantasies which absorb him, but visions rather, involving fresh problems and new possibilities in painting, ideas which continually exercise his mind.

JACK HUMPHREY (1901-   )

A Painter's Painter [1]

JACK WELDON HUMPHREY was born in Saint John, N.B., in 1901, and has painted there most of his adult life. There is no doubt that an inward compulsion has driven him on through poverty and initial lack of recognition to his present position of distinction. Humphrey has to paint, and his devotion to the subject matter provided by the city of Saint John is the measure of his singleness of purpose. It is a strange, inscrutable city, set on bleak and rocky hills, patterned with an excruciating mid-Victorian architecture, and washed by the ebb and flow of Fundy tides round the base of rotting piles and sagging docks. Yet it can produce, even in the unpainted wooden jungle of Main Street, and the sleazy tumbledown shacks of " Indian Town," a melancholy beauty which Humphrey has made peculiarly his own.

Humphrey attended Mount Allison University for a short while, but was forced through illness to abandon his studies there. Later he went to the School of the Museum of Fine Arts, Boston, and then to Charles Hawthorne's classes at the School of the National Academy of Design in New York. Subsequently, through private benefactors, he spent nine months travelling in Europe, and, returning to Saint John at the outset of the depression, he struggled through that gloomy period in an atmosphere highly dispiriting to the creative artist.

" When the economic depression relaxes," he wrote at this time, " unless some favourable opportunity presents itself, I have the exceedingly unpleasant prospect of returning to some form of unskilled and ill-paid labour at night in New York City in order to attempt to support the thus impoverished efforts of contributing to art and civilisation by day. Having existed in this way for about five years and to the limit of endurance, I do not speak without knowledge when I say that it hinders accomplishment and lowers morale."

But artists are extraordinarily tough. Humphrey did not return to New York ; he stayed in Saint John, and by about 1935 had already begun to achieve national recognition. He has never done anything else but paint. Unlike many other painters, he has never attempted to mix art with other methods of earning a livelihood ; nor, though he has had his ups and downs, has he ever succumbed to the temptation to be regional for mere regionalism's sake.

Humphrey is apt to explain his fascination for Saint John with the laconic phrase : " A bunch of us got stuck here in the depression." But this is only

[1] This essay has been contributed by Graham McInnes.

XIII. JACK HUMPHREY (1901-   )
"Portrait of a Girl"
Oil: 36″ × 28″. *New Brunswick Museum, Saint John, N.B.*

a small part of the explanation. Fundamentally, Humphrey loves his native city and is not really at home when he is away from it—as those who have seen his Mexican paintings will readily admit. For he sums up the city with his sensitive moods of mournfulness and melancholy, and although he is greater than what he paints, he is still basically of it ; which brings us to the truism that the artist finds and displays the universal in his own particular background. That is why, although one certainly need not see Saint John to recognise that Humphrey is a fine painter, it helps if one can watch him at work on his native heath.

The artists in Saint John live and work in old office buildings in the warehouse section of the city. Humphrey's apartment is a second-floor "walk-up" at 108 Prince William Street, within a stone's-throw of his fellow-artists in similar quarters. The entrance is like that of an old-fashioned lawyer's office, and the stairs, though they creak, are of rich dark woods no longer seen in this era of plastic and glass : woods that reek of the great sea-trading days when Saint John was the fourth city in Canada.

In his quarters, Humphrey from time to time entertains his friends and fellow-artists. Occasionally there will be a magnificent meal of roast bear. Sometimes he will play the violin to the accompaniment of an upright grand or "box" piano of a type rarely seen now, but common enough in old Maritime homes. There will be plenty of talk and argument, but little from Humphrey. He prefers mostly to sit with his impressive bulk slumped in a chair, his contemplative blue eyes sunk beneath his high forehead with its wisps of grizzled hair, and about his lips a half smile as if enjoying some inner joke. He does not talk much about his painting ; he prefers to listen, and to paint ; he remains curiously aloof, monolithic and introvert.

His studio is a genial clutter of chests, old canvases and water-colours, and here and there objects with which he is experimenting in his recent trend towards a more abstract treatment ; smooth silver-grey driftwood, pitchers, sea-shells and pottery. Before the tall window looking out across the harbour to West Saint John he has cleared himself a small space in which to work. His field sketching is often done from a venerable 1932 sedan which he refers to as " the old jalopy." In it he camps, watching the passers-by on Main Street, the Canadian Pacific banging over the cross-town tracks and the tide nudging the boats higher at the foot of Market Street. Or he may park the jalopy at the entrance to one of the docks and plant his camp stool at some point of vantage whence the endless rearrangement of the sharp edges and dissolving planes of the city can be caught—usually across water. For relaxation, which with Humphrey means painting, there is his camp on a lake a few miles out of the city.

What is the achievement? Humphrey is at his best in his apparently inconsequential but, in reality, carefully worked out and sensitively felt water-colours of Saint John and its harbour. His method in these is simple and direct. Working with charcoal or pen and ink he will suggest a few significant lines ; these are then enveloped by a quick series of washes or sudden dabs of paint, all closely related tonally. This method of working distils a mood which evokes a sense of sadness and of *memento mori* that is unique and entirely personal to him. It is not aggressive painting ; there lies about it a sort of lyric disenchantment with the visible world, and a retreat into certain timeless values to be seen in the subtleties of space and mood in his compositions.

In his larger oils, though they are more worked over and more complex both in conception and in realisation, one senses the same evasive sadness, as in this *Portrait of a Girl* (Plate XIII). His still lifes and his figure painting become, at their best, almost monumental ; and if they appear to be static it is only in the same deceptive way that a Chardin still life may appear to be static.

Recently Humphrey wrote : " Once a painter has learned enough about his craft it is of the utmost importance that he bring all the activity of his perception, of his will and his instinct to making his work live with qualities discovered within and without. So with me, when painting has gone well it has been the sought-out subject, usually from objective Nature or human model, transformed and rebuilt in terms of the painter's craft and effective visual means. These latter are manifest in character : thick space, colour, variety, proportion, movement and all the rest. My immediate concern seems to be with ' What colour and where ? ' "

In a short-wave broadcast from Canada to the United Kingdom, he added : " It is because I like what I have discovered in this part of Canada that I could not reduce painting to the doodling that has no reference to seen things. However, merely quaint pictures of recognisable subjects are not enough. We have to go deeper. We must go realistically, with all possible resources of painting, into the imaginative spirit of the land and the people that are at hand."

Humphrey is fundamentally a romantic working with classic restraint and in low-keyed colour values. He is a lyricist singing in a minor key ; and it is sometimes hard to separate the melancholy of Saint John from the melancholy of Humphrey. But his subtle quietist approach carries with it the reward of lasting appreciation.

Recognition of his talent among his fellow-craftsmen is high. He has been at various times vice-president of the Canadian Society of Painters in Water Colour, regional representative of the Canadian Society of Graphic Art and a director of the Canadian Group of Painters. But such honours are merely the outward symbols of a feeling, pretty general among Canadian artists, that Humphrey is that rarest of creatures, a painter's painter. That this makes matters difficult for him in the commercial sense need hardly be laboured here. He made up his mind on that score almost twenty years ago when he stated : " The ideal to be kept in mind is that art should be understood for its own sake. As every artist knows, art adapted for commerce and rewarded by commerce, however useful or well carried out, is of secondary significance. The fine arts flow inevitably from the æsthetic spirit and are designed to evoke a spiritual reaction."

LOUIS MUHLSTOCK (1904-   )

A Spontaneous Naturalism

IN the many large drawings he does of the nude, Louis Muhlstock seeks to depict the sculptural qualities of torso and limbs. So much does he concentrate on such studies—for example, during one winter he finished at least one large drawing of a nude figure every day for seven months—that his friends often wonder why he has not gone on to model in clay or even carve in stone. But he seems content to realise such forms to the highest degree he can by means of line alone.

Strangely enough, when he turns to painting, it is not the colour of light playing on flesh which appears to move him most ; it is rather the atmosphere of sun and shade in the green depths of a Canadian forest or the contrast of brick and masonry and foliage along a Montreal street. In his canvases, which are rarely of figures or faces, mostly of landscapes, he works directly from Nature ; in fact, nearly all his finished paintings—they average about 30 by 36 inches in size—can best be described as outdoor sketches. They are all rapidly composed impressions of certain familiar scenes which attract his eye and brush, not once, but time and time again. There is, for example, one particular patch of woods, penetrated by a winding path, near the farm he visits in the Laurentians, which he has painted perhaps a score and more of times.

Brought to Montreal from Eastern Europe at the age of seven by his parents, who were poor Jewish immigrants from Galicia, he grew up in the slum and tenement areas of the city. After he had finished high school, he obtained a job as a book-keeper. But he had a craving to draw and paint, which could not be downed, so he began to attend various night classes in art. The instruction provided by them was, however, only perfunctory, and at them he says he learned nothing. Dissatisfied, he began to save money to go to Paris. In 1928, when he was twenty-four, he set out for that city and there for four years he studied in the studio of Louis-François Biloul. Most Canadian artists who travel to Paris, go there for advanced training or to work independently. But Louis was a mere beginner when he arrived in that city of artistic sophistication ; while there, he sought simply to learn the rudiments of his craft. He stuck closely to the classes of the school and it was not until his fourth and final year that he commenced to notice or take any interest at all in the wider world of contemporary art.

Returning to Montreal in 1931, during the midst of the slump, he took to frequenting Fletcher's Fields, an open, rather unkempt park, where the most ragged and depressed of the unemployed spent their days. Here he did many drawings of men lying asleep on the grass or sitting staring morosely into space. Because of this period of his work, when he went also to those overnight refuges for the out-of-work, to draw naked men grouped under showers or waiting outside in the snow to gain admittance, he came to be known by some as an artist of proletarian significance. But the social content of this early work of his was only incidental to his human sympathies in general.

Muhlstock saves everything he does, even to the merest notations he makes on scraps of paper. At the same time, there are few who buy his drawings, for while many collectors are interested in the fresh colours he so enthusiastically displays in his canvases, only a handful pay the attention they should to the cooler virtues of line and contour which he expresses so ably in black and white. As a result, he has enormous piles of drawings stored in his studio, and when you visit him, he will go back over them until he finds the drawings of the unemployed. But when he talks about these, he is more likely to show you how he finally managed, after many preliminary sketches, to sum up, in a few strong and sure lines, the posture of some sleeping figure sprawled over crumpled newspapers on the greensward, than he is to comment on the mood or background of the subject itself.

As for the few paintings he has done of slum streets, in quarters near where he lived as a child, these appear to be strangely detached studies with their emphasis mostly on the formalism of blank, brick walls and broken pavement in deserted alleys. Yet even so, they possess emotional overtones which the painter himself may not consciously have intended them to convey. Also he has done a series of interiors of gaunt, empty houses. Looking at them, one feels that, wishing to submit himself to the discipline of pure abstraction, but not being of a disposition to create more cerebral and non-objective designs of planes and simplified textures, he seized instead upon compositions of this kind, as and when he saw them in the visible world. For example, he once painted a completely empty room, seen through an open door, and then afterwards the same room from within looking out towards a decayed hall and broken stairway. Yet his lyrical approach to Nature was such that the starkness of such scenes could not hold him for long. Recently, he has found more delight in depicting some of the older residential streets of Montreal, filled as in this painting, *Street Corner, Montreal* (Plate 54), with great elm trees behind which rise solid rows of brick or stone buildings.

When one sees compositions such as this, one agrees with Robert Ayre, who wrote recently in *Northern Review* : " You feel that there is sap in his trees, that the earth is alive for him, that in all its seasons and moods it is an experience worth having, and sharing. In other words, he paints the earth—and the sunny city streets, which have no undertone of bitterness, however poor they may be—with the warmth of affection."

During the war years, he felt the need for participation as an artist in the stirring, striving events of the time. He decided that he would go out by himself, without benefit of commission or payment, and paint the hurried action and life of the war production plants. The first visit he made was to the United Shipyards in Montreal. There, he says, as soon as he saw the riveters working in teams on the plates of the great towering structures of the hulls, he knew that this was what he wanted, that he need go no further. He came back every morning for months. The men soon accepted his presence among them in the grime and noise and dust ; they took his painting as a recognition of their own duties and tasks. The more Muhlstock remained among them, the more he became interested in each detail of their operations. He ended up by studying the strength of the grip of a man's hands on a riveting machine, and he made one fine composition, of which he is very proud, of such hands alone.

A similar need for participation can be sensed in the enthusiasm with which he throws himself into any projects which relate to the position and the acceptance of the artist in society. " The painter's job," he states categorically, " does not end when the work of art is produced." He is willing, when such issues arise, to write vehement letters to newspapers or cogently phrased articles for magazines.

In particular, any censorship of the nude in art will incite him to wield his pen in aroused anger against such puritanical refusal to see beauty in the human form. " Throughout the ages and all down the history of art from the early cave drawings and earliest known carvings, the human figure has predominated among all subjects chosen by artists," he wrote once in an article in *Canadian Art* on the question of the refusal of a certain western Canadian art gallery to show a particular nude painting, and he added: " Here, for lack of courage on the part of the artist and for want of encouragement and understanding on the part of the public in general, this great chain of continuity in the arts has been broken and we turn almost entirely to landscape and still life for inspiration. Is this because the Canadian figure is not as beautiful as the Greek, Italian or the central European ? As for artists, I say to them the battle of the nudes has been going on for a long time in this ' beau pays,' and it is bound to continue for some time to come, so let us, as painters and sculptors, meet the challenge. We can do this by painting and moulding and carving the human figure, with the deepest love of form and colour, and with the greatest respect for mankind."

ALFRED PELLAN (1906-   )

Magnifico of Modernism

AS has been related in the essay on John Lyman, a wider appreciation of what is meant by " living art," in terms of modern painting, was being actively promoted in Montreal after 1939 by the Contemporary Arts Society. During this period, a secondary, but almost equally important influence was provided by the presence of various painters and critics of prominence, who had come to Canada as refugees from war-torn France. Among them was Fernand Léger, the neo-cubist master, who attracted quite a following while in Montreal, although he did not remain there for long. Another refugee was that highly cultured priest of the Dominican order, Father M. A. Couturier, who is well known to-day in Europe for his recent association with Henri Matisse in the building and decoration of a chapel at Vence in the south of France.

Father Couturier, while he was in Montreal, tried to bring into Roman Catholic intellectual circles in the province of Quebec a greater awareness and appreciation of the principles of modern expression in art. In his public and college lectures, of which he gave many, he emphasised his belief that in the western world each age since the Renaissance has produced a universal school of painting, and that for our age this was and is the School of Paris. It is a school, he added, which partakes of no special geographical characteristics ; its principles are based rather on " this spirit and this life of extreme conscience and extreme liberty, one implying the other." He also organised several exhibitions of Canadian art in which he sought to demonstrate his thesis that " in so far as they have been original, personal or independent, Canadian artists have revealed and still do reveal these same qualities of the life and of the spirit as used to be dominant in Paris." For these he drew largely on the works of members of the Contemporary Arts Society. Before he left, he published in Montreal, under the title, *Chronicles*, a book of philosophical and religious reflections. Included in this was an essay on painting in Canada, in which Couturier criticised both our academic and regionalist schools of painting and advocated that recognition be given instead to those few artists " whose work came from the deepest, the most secret and the most personal sources of their being."

Enthusiasms so engendered, either through the activities of the Contemporary Arts Society or through the writings and lectures of Father Couturier, however, did not always spread as rapidly as might have been expected. Various struggles, both major and minor, took place before those

95

strongholds of orthodoxy, the museums and art schools of Montreal, were prepared to accept any new dispensation in the arts.

The first great conflict between the upholders of academic traditions and these younger men who believed in the need for a more personal expression in painting came not over the exhibitions of the Contemporary Arts Society or as a reaction to the crusade led by Father Couturier, but rather over the rights of a young painter, Alfred Pellan, to teach at the Ecole des Beaux-Arts according to his own lights and without hindrance from bureaucratic authority.

Pellan, after a sojourn of fourteen years in Paris, had come back in 1940 to his native province. A government scholarship had originally taken him to France, but he had remained afterwards to work on his own, and in Paris he had soon achieved a certain degree of prominence, remarkable enough for a man so young. Several French museums bought his paintings and in 1935 he won first prize in the Première Exposition d'Art Mural.

Upon his return, a retrospective showing of over eighty of his paintings and drawings was held both in Quebec City and in Montreal. " He brings an almost unforgivable exuberance and sense of health into our otherwise anaemic artistic circles," exclaimed one critic upon viewing this exhibition. In Montreal, the *éclat* caused by his more sensational offerings was tremendous, and his painting at once became the talk of the town. The younger generation looked upon him as a brilliant magnifico of the arts, dispensing a wealth of resources in decorative panels of riotous colours and of involved forms. But to many of the older generation, his work appeared puzzling, dangerous almost. A sort of lone wolf, he remained at first aloof from local contacts and took little part even in the activities of his fellow-painters. But so strong was the impact of his art that a rallying of the more vocal forces of independent painting in Quebec soon took place round the banner of his name and reputation.

The struggles in the Ecole des Beaux-Arts arose from the inner life of the school itself, which for many years had been languishing in an academic torpor brought on by increasing rigidities in administration. This conflict, after smouldering for a year, came into the open in 1945, when a riot broke out at the opening of the school's annual exhibition. A number of students began to cry, " A bas Maillard ! à bas l'Académisme ! " and then they distributed cards attacking the director, Charles Maillard. The immediate cause of this outbreak was given great publicity at the time. It lay in the refusal of the director to hang two paintings submitted by students of Pellan, one a painting of a nude in which pubic hair was shown, a degree of realism which had not apparently been allowed previously in the school, and the second a stylised treatment, " à la moderne," as Maillard called it, of the Last Supper. The director, it appeared, had sought advice on the pictures from a cleric attached to the office of the Archbishop. The newspapers, of course,

XIV. STANLEY COSGROVE (1912-   )
" Still Life with Milk Dish "
Oil: 16″ × 26″. *National Gallery of Canada, Ottawa*

seized upon the attendant circumstances of the riot with relish. Some few writers, however, were astute enough to go on to investigate the administration of the school, and they soon found the main issue at stake was that of bureaucratic controls as opposed to more personal methods of teaching. As agitation in the press mounted, it became obvious that Maillard's regime could count upon little support in high places, and so he resigned. Since then the school has been fairly completely rehabilitated and two other fine artists, Stanley Cosgrove and Jacques de Tonnancour, now teach there as well as Pellan.

The memory of this quarrel, aptly titled by one French-Canadian newspaper "La Querelle des pompiers et des artistes vivantes," has been wittily recorded by Pellan in a large canvas, *Surprise Académique* (Plate 57). This picture is typical of his mature style. In it we see grouped together a score of references related to this dispute, some realistic, some symbolical. As in a contemporary poem, one needs to possess a key to comprehend all the details. But some of them are obvious enough. The jester in the centre is the former director, and to the right there is a small Trojan horse from which the large figure of an artist, representing Pellan, is emerging. And, of course, at the top there are a few " wheels within wheels."

When you first meet Pellan you realise at once how impossible it is for him to fit into any pattern of white-collar formality. He is short and stocky, the true French-Canadian artisan in type and appearance. Meet him in his work clothes on the street and you might mistake him for a master carpenter or a shop foreman.

The introspective approach of many modern artists, the delicacy of touch of the easel painter who concentrates on creating a world within the confines of a small frame, does not appeal to Pellan, even although at an earlier stage of his career he did a few still lifes which, as the one shown in colour (Plate XV) proves, were as close to Bonnard as they were to the cubists. He confesses quite candidly that he feels himself to be simply a highly skilled workman who should be hired on commission to do decorative murals, textile and rug designs and the like. That he doesn't get many such commissions in Canada irks him greatly, for, as he says, his greatest joy in creation was when he was once hired years ago to embellish, in this way, every wall, from the bedrooms to living-room and kitchen, of a large country house in Brittany. In Montreal, he has had to be content with doing a few stage sets, some book illustrations, and murals for installation in the Canadian Embassies in Rio de Janiero and Paris.

The course of his career has been well summarised by the collector, Dr. Paul Dumas, who wrote several years ago : " At first, he produced solely representational works, mainly austere and monochromatic portraits which remind us of the beautiful heads of Derain and of the early Bérard. Later on, influenced by Braque, Juan Gris and Bonnard, he painted a series of still lifes, extremely rich in tones and personal in the arrangement of forms, which mark a peak in his art. Going further, he assimilated other influences, Picasso, Miro, Masson, Klee and Léger, and turned gradually towards non-representative painting, either intermingling so-called abstract patterns in objective painting, or limiting himself to the non-objective vocabulary. Since his return here, after a transitory try at figure painting, he has concentrated on ambitious, semi-abstract compositions, synthetic in conception and in which graphic and plastic elements are sometimes ambiguously interwoven, but that possess, none the less, a sort of savage grandeur. Pellan has undoubtedly proved himself to be a force in Canadian painting."

Some critics complain that his work shows too much the direct influence of half a dozen of the more famous masters of the School of Paris, to which one can only reply that, of course, it does—for he has a great talent for absorbing and using what others have found before him. But his forceful personality has for the most part enabled him to pass relatively unharmed down these paths of easy virtuosity.

Removed from all that fullness of life and that richness of artistic contacts which were his when he lived in Paris, where he knew Picasso, Miro and Juan Gris, he experienced upon his return to Canada, for the first time in his career, the deeper meaning of that " drama of solitude " upon which creative painting is so often based. As a result, he seems to be discovering more clearly to-day what he wants to say himself, and he says it occasionally in canvases of unmistakable power.

One such is that large work of almost mural size, *Femmes d'une Pomme*, which has been hung recently in several important exhibitions. Also some of his newer water-colours, such as *Les Iles de la Nuit* (Plate 58), are quite personal to himself. One should note here that while Pellan vigorously opposes the " automatiste " form of surrationalism developed by Borduas and his followers, he is willing to use, as in this water-colour, the subconscious in his own way. The raw material of surrealism, he has been quoted as saying, " should still be filtered through the conscious mind. The painter should be like a fisherman who keeps some fish that he brings to the surface and throws the rest back."

He has already, through the impact of his art, sown fertile seeds which have taken firm root in the artistic soil of Quebec. As his young friend and colleague, Jacques de Tonnancour, explains : " In order to be resurrected after these centuries of slumber . . . French Canadian art needed . . . a vigorous blow from the outside," and that blow was delivered by Pellan who through his work has demonstrated to scores of younger painters that beauty is something to be " produced, not simply reproduced."

XV. ALFRED PELLAN (1906-   )
"Still Life"
Oil: 21″ × 31″. Musée de la Province de Québec, Quebec City

PAUL-ÉMILE BORDUAS (1905-   )

Surrationalism in a Quebec Setting

FRENCH-CANADIAN culture has moved and continues to move in a hesitant path between the live realities of North American life and the limitations of its own imposed traditions, inherited from pre-revolutionary France. But more and more the universal ferment of the twentieth century slowly insinuates itself into the thoughts and habits of Quebec. Students and artists and travellers move constantly between French Canada and New York and Paris. They return, their minds assailed with perplexing doubts or filled with freshly found enthusiasms. Sometimes, as a result, inner tensions build up but remain hidden, only finally to explode in manifestations which may shake, even if they do not move, the well-built walls of provincial orthodoxy.

Such an incident occurred in 1948 when a group of younger painters, and writers, mainly friends or followers of Paul-Émile Borduas, calling themselves " automatistes," published a manifesto entitled *Refus Global*. The assumption made by these artists in their attack on existing educational and artistic institutions in Quebec was akin to that of the philosophical anarchists, for they reasoned that human personality was always in itself good until corrupted by the deforming power of fixed rules and organised authority. To them " automatisme " implied the discarding of orthodox restrictions and the creating of something pristine and fresh in artistic expression by purely intuitive means. Only through instinctive composition, they declared, could one move towards a more essentially human and universal art.

For Borduas and his colleagues to add that this path was the only one which any artists in Quebec aspiring to independence could take was certainly a challenging statement. Yet it was a free and honest expression of opinion, and they backed it up by quoting certain well-known surrationalist views on æsthetics which had been promulgated previously in France by André Breton and others. It was a manifesto, however, which by the very vehemence of its expression, invited retaliation ; and retaliation came at once, for no sooner was it published than Borduas, who had been teaching at the state-supported Ecole du Meuble in Montreal, was discharged from his post by ministerial decree.

Who then is this supposedly wild-eyed anarchist who has so startled the bureaucratic dove-cotes of Quebec ?

Borduas is a native French-Canadian of rural stock, who was born and brought up in one of the most placid spots to be found in the Quebec countryside, that is the village of St. Hilaire on the Richelieu River. This is a pleasant and prosperous community, comfortably situated beside a wooded mountain which rises in isolated beauty above the farmlands of the plain. Here there lived when Borduas was a boy, and still does live, a certain Ozias Leduc, a modest painter of mellow landscapes and fastidious still lifes, who also executed piously conceived religious panels and murals for the parish churches of the region. The young Borduas became first an admirer of Leduc, then an active disciple, and was soon taking lessons from him. Later, leaving his native village, he went to the Ecole des Beaux-Arts in Montreal ; after some years of study there, he moved on to the Ateliers d'Art Sacré in Paris, where his master was that gifted but restrained and intelligently conservative painter, Maurice Denis. Borduas was a willing student, and he returned to Canada equipped with a considerable knowledge of his craft. He might have ended up as a specialist in ecclesiastical art, only, as he says, no one bothered to give him any commissions. So he gave up his attempts to be a decorator of churches, and took instead a post as a teacher of children's art classes in Montreal schools.

Of his experiences during these years following his return to Canada in 1932, he writes : " In a state of great destitution, without friends who could follow my thoughts or to whom I could talk about the forms of art I loved, I kept seeking the reasons why it was impossible to fit myself into the framework of society . . ." At the same time he adds : " I made one after the other, the following discoveries : fauvism, cubism, surrealism." He learned much now himself from the children he was teaching, for, as he explains : " The children, whom I never lost sight of, opened wide before me the door leading to surrealism, to automatic writing. The most perfect condition of the art of painting was finally unveiled for me." Here he uses the term surrealism more in the sense of surrationalism, that is of some instinctive act of creation, existing beneath, but at the same time going beyond, conscious reasoning powers.

As he liberated his spirit, so his feeling of isolation departed. He began to find friends of a kindred nature, " half-liberated men and women " of whom he had never previously " suspected the existence in Montreal." John Lyman introduced him into the ranks of the Contemporary Arts Society. Also, an old acquaintance, the Dominican, Father H. M. Couturier, who had studied fresco together with him years before at Chaillons in France, was now in Montreal and, through the exhibitions which Couturier arranged and in which his pictures were included, Borduas received additional support.

The story of how Borduas developed and expanded his stimulating, although controversial, methods of teaching, after he had been given a post as painting instructor in 1937 at the Ecole du Meuble, a school of furniture crafts and design, and of the widening breach which opened later between himself and the administration of the school, are all outlined in most readable detail in an autobiographical essay, *Projections Libérantes*, which he published in 1949. His ability to clarify his æsthetic principles in writing, in sentences often both forceful and richly phrased, reveals a talent which one might wish could be equally displayed at times by some of our more reticent English-speaking painters. Outside of Montreal, artists in Canada seem too inclined to devote their surplus energies entirely to duties of professional organisation or to those vague generalities of action which they call " the development of sound public relations for the arts." They too often forget that arguments and discussions, ably led and waged, between conflicting æsthetic principles and creeds can help to fertilise the growing culture of a nation.

To appreciate Borduas as a painter, one must first understand that slow expansion towards freedom which marked the earlier growth of his art. At first his work was somewhat meticulous and confined ; in fact, he did not really achieve any measure of original power until after 1937.

He then began to apply pigment, at least in the initial stages of his compositions, as an " automatic " gesture. There was nothing new in this principle, of course. He was not going even as far in this direction as did one of those ancient Chinese masters of whom it is related that, when beginning his compositions, he would dip his hair in a bowl of ink and shake his locks over a large sheet of paper ; then, where and as the ink had spattered, he would seek and find the elements on which to base his imaginary renderings of trees and forests and mountains.

Borduas does not follow such supremely surrational methods. Yet he does let the first instinctively directed strokes of his brush determine the initial pattern of his compositions.

In his first work of this nature, he continued to retain certain representational concepts. Meditating upon the vague beginnings of shape and form, as they flowed from his brush, he would go on to decide what references to landscape or figures or objects could be built up out of them. In such a way he created his *La Femme au Bijou* (Plate 62) and this mysterious horse from some lower or outer world, *La Cavale Infernale* (Plate 60). In other words, he didn't plan in advance to depict such subjects—they grew rather out of his canvas as he worked upon it.

In 1941 he stopped doing oils for a while and, taking up gouache as a medium, he began to produce, with even greater emphasis than before on instinctive composition, a series of completely non-objective paintings. " You have found in your gouaches that plastic purity which makes painting what it is," wrote Jacques de Tonnancour in *La Nouvelle Revue* ; while Marcel Parizeau, in his introduction to an exhibition of contemporary Canadian painting held in Andover, Massachusetts, in 1942, described them as : " This series of fifty unexpected gouaches, produced spontaneously . . . a kind of waking dream which guards within its boundaries an accumulation of strength and experience, which qualities make their presence felt automatically, as a reflex action. . . ."

Since that date, Borduas, using this same reflex response, has been doing larger compositions of oil on canvas. To-day he no longer seeks, at any stage of his work, to bring representational references into his pictures. What he paints now are abstractions, pure and simple. But after he has finished such compositions, he still sometimes gives them titles which tend to call up more concrete imagery, as in the recent *Les Parachutes Végétaux* (Plate XVI).

As a result of the strong appeal which both Borduas and Pellan, in their diverse ways, make to the younger generation of French-Canadian artists, we now find a division of effort springing up within the modern movement in Quebec.

"The young," as Borduas writes, "have taken violently held sides." At the right of the contemporary movement is a type of art related to cubism, with its accent on static construction based on reasonable, well-defined theories derived largely from contemporary French painting. Those, who take this as their gospel, have put the name of Pellan on their banner. At the left is another doctrine, which Borduas defines as a dynamism of fluid composition, practised by artists who run all the risks of uncertain discovery in seeking new forms of plastic expression derived from the subconscious. Here, the leader adopted by the young is Borduas himself. In between, of course, there are those who, like Stanley Cosgrove, utter "a plague on both your houses" and go their own more reserved but equally purposeful and independent ways.

XVI. PAUL-ÉMILE BORDUAS (1905-   )
" Les Parachutes Végétaux "
Oil: $32\frac{1}{4}'' \times 43\frac{1}{4}''$. *National Gallery of Canada, Ottawa*

STANLEY COSGROVE (1911-   )

Towards a Contemporary Classicism

IN many respects, Stanley Cosgrove can be defined as one of the most North American of Canadian painters. Although his name is Irish, his background is that of French-speaking Montreal. After finishing his studies in Montreal, he was awarded a scholarship which enabled him to spend four years in Mexico. In that country he became interested in fresco painting and worked under the great José Clemente Orozco. But the social dynamism which we associate with so much of contemporary Mexican production has so far exerted little or no overt influence upon his own work. He brought back, it is true, from his Mexican sojourn a few sober studies of Indians and some slightly gayer ones of their festival processions, also a number of paintings on the theme of the crucifixion, but in the years since then he has concentrated upon more placid subjects—the faces of women, trees in woodland glades or still-life compositions of fruit and plates and a pitcher on a table.

Freed from the dogma of Canadian regionalism, freed also from any too close subservience to modern French masters, he presents us with a personal art of discreet independence and vigorous, if subdued, strength. Working in a modern idiom, but with classical restraint, he has built up his own dry but delicate style in oils.

Coming to study art somewhat later than is usual—he was twenty-six when he first started classes at the Ecole des Beaux-Arts in Montreal—he, nevertheless, felt such an urge to develop himself thoroughly as a painter that, although it meant living often on the slimmest of incomes, he went on, after he had finished at the Beaux-Arts, to take instruction in figure painting from Edwin Holgate. His early work was derivative and impressionist ; then for a time he used colours surprisingly similar to those we associate with the canvases of the Belgian painter, James Ensor. Finally, towards the end of his seven years as a student, he began to develop a more personal style, marked by low-keyed but warm tonalities and dry and even-surfaced textures. One of the first works he did of this nature was the *Portrait of a Young Woman* (Plate 55), which was painted shortly before he went to Mexico.

At this time he was beginning to develop an enthusiasm for the work of certain French masters, such as Braque and Rouault. Certainly, when he applied for and received a Province of Quebec scholarship in 1939 he had every intention of going to Paris to continue his studies. In fact, he would have left for France that summer if he had not been asked to put on a one-man show at the Provincial Museum in Quebec—an enviable distinction for one who was still a student—and the preparation of this exhibition delayed his sailing. Then war broke out, and he was advised that the scholarship would no longer be tenable in France and that he should plan to hold it on this continent instead, preferably in the United States. But after two months in New York, he and his young wife decided that they were not happy there, so they packed up and bought tickets to Mexico City. It was a decision Cosgrove never regretted.

Shortly after his arrival in Mexico, with its stimulating mixture of Indian and Spanish cultures, he decided that he wanted to learn the art of fresco as it had been revived there in recent years. He particularly admired Orozco, but he was told that this prominent painter did not take pupils. Nothing daunted, Cosgrove approached him through friends, and asked him, if he could not work as an apprentice assistant, without pay, on any new mural commission Orozco received. The master gave his consent, and soon the Canadian was busy in a great hall where a fresco was being created. Cosgrove had little at first to do but make guiding measurements on the wall, but then after some months, he was allowed to draw in and paint a few of the more minor details himself. In fresco you must paint on the wet plaster with fast and even brush strokes ; you may not falter, for it is impossible to do any major corrections or over-painting. He was given an area in which the position of a long link of great chains was roughly indicated ; Orozco told him not to look at the small guiding sketches, but rather simply to think of chains, and to go ahead and paint quickly. Working thus, he was forced to drop all timidity of approach.

From this experience, Cosgrove claims he brought back to his own easel painting a new assurance, an honest directness which he had not previously had. These qualities first became evident in the many still lifes he did in his own small studio in Mexico City. In addition, he made drawings from the model, also sometimes he went to the streets and market-places for his subjects or to the brittle landscapes of the upland plateau with their cactus and yucca.

After his return to Canada, he concentrated at first on still-life compositions. These are often in gay colours, although never in brilliant ones ; also the brighter touches, when they appear, are usually muted by a cool mixture of background tones. Sometimes the forms are distorted, sometimes they are more closely representational in outline.

He has no desire to relate his paintings directly to objective reality. This can be seen in his method of composing landscapes. On his visits to the countryside, he makes a number of rough pencil sketches, to which he adds a few colour notations. Months later, in his studio, taking up these brief notes, he will begin to compose, with only indirect reference to them, certain of his characteristic studies of trees dispersed in an open glade. Recently, during the course of one year, he did as many as a dozen finished paintings from such notes, each one of them mutations on the same theme of sere and sombre trunks and branches, devoid for the most part of foliage, scenes existing without reference to any exactitude of time or place.

Particularly in his landscapes, but also in most of his figure studies, the colours he prefers are of the earth—the umbers, greys and ochres. He has never had a liking for the texture of canvas ; he prefers the smooth firmness of masonite.

His method of working is so closely related to the results he obtains that it deserves description in detail. He begins by mounting the masonite sheet on a wooden frame and then he carefully covers its surface with a white sizing. Drawing in the main outlines of his composition, he brushes in the background tones in light warm colours. Afterwards, he works up the structure by adding darker tones of the same or closely allied colours, brushing in at the same time secondary details of contour. Later, he may apply a few brighter touches, a stroke of rich blue for the fold of a dress and a pure vermilion to emphasise the line of a buckle or a belt. Never does he use paint thickly ; he always puts it on thinly, in strokes that are almost transparent. This is because he feels that the heavy, oily pigment, *la matiére*, so delighted in by many artists, is something which can lend itself too easily to empty emotionalism.

More profound qualities of harmony and equilibrium of space and colour relationships are what he seeks, and, when he achieves them, he wants them to stand on their own merits, without having to compete, as he says, with what is often merely superficial and facile " brush-work." He also avoids the other extreme of smooth, glossy surfaces or of meticulously built-up glazes. What he obtains, rather, is a dry, but yet curiously warm, mat finish. At the same time, the fluidity of oil as a medium allows him to keep a lightness to his surfaces which distinguish them from the more obviously flat and opaque textures of paintings done in gouache or similar media. The cool delicacy of these tones of his, with their translucent effects, reminds one much of the atmosphere of late autumn in Canada ; for example, the background colours in many of his portraits recall the faint tints of those yellowish leaves which, with a touch of scarlet and ochre still visible in their tracery, often carpet the ground in late October.

One wonders how directly this technique of his in oils may be related to his experiences with fresco. One thing is certain, his prime ambition is some day to be able to obtain commissions to paint frescoes in Canada. He points out that a few such murals have recently been done in Quebec churches by a technically able but uninspired Italian artist whose work unfortunately falls into the pattern of the most saccharine models of nineteenth-century ecclesiastical art. Cosgrove hopes that his associates and himself will be able to effect some reforms here, and, as a first step in doing so, he has organised classes in fresco, under the ægis of the Ecole des Beaux-Arts in Montreal ; these have already met with a fairly enthusiastic response.

Much of the discipline he has subjected himself to in his constantly renewed interpretations of the same familiar groupings of small objects on a table has been a necessary prelude, he states, to arriving at a mature understanding of all the intricacies and subtleties of formal composition. The ideal he strives for, he hastens to explain, is a much broader one than " the composure of still life " and " form for its own sake." He looks forward to the day when, as he says, he will be able, in all honesty, to introduce a greater depth of human content into his art. By that he means he does not want to rush into what he feels are more social and also higher realisations of art without adequate preparation. While he admires the motives of those painters who go directly to factories to describe workmen on the job or who tackle enthusiastically such typical scenes of Canadian life as children skating on outdoor rinks, he nevertheless maintains that he, for one, will not attempt such involved and intensely alive themes until he is certain he can give them some spiritual and æsthetic as well as documentary validity.

JACQUES de TONNANCOUR (1917-   )

Youth and the Inner Man

TO create new beauty on canvas, one must first " take nature and twist its neck." That, on the face of it, is a desperate statement ; yet it explains exactly how Jacques de Tonnancour felt when he tried to paint the supreme beauty of Brazilian landscape. Before such scenes as those surrounding the harbour of Rio de Janeiro, compositions already completely and immutably arranged by Nature, he had either to reconcile himself to painting " picture post-cards in oil," or to find some more personal method of abstracting the more essential and plastic elements of these scenes. Of his experiences in painting these landscapes, he concludes : " This dramatic tension between what is called subject and painter tortured me as much as it attracted me."

Having struggled through such perplexities, this young Montreal artist returned to Canada fortified with a deeper awareness of the demands of creative painting. There should be, he claims, " death and transfiguration " in each work of art, " death of the natural elements and their resurrection transfigured in the painting."

De Tonnancour was only twenty-eight in 1945 when the Brazilian Government granted him a scholarship which enabled him to spend a year in Rio de Janeiro. But he had already attracted considerable attention both in Canada and elsewhere for his fine and sensitive drawings and his confidently painted figure studies. Earlier that year, a Brazilian critic, Geraldo Ferraz, in his review of a large exhibition of contemporary Canadian art, which was then showing in Rio, went out of his way to praise this young artist. " The two great names," he said, " are Alfred Pellan and Jacques de Tonnancour," and he added: "The emphasis of the painting of Pellan, in discovering new worlds, is justifiable, but we find in de Tonnancour other things, more intimate, profound, perhaps even greater."

One canvas mentioned by Ferraz, *Les Gants de Filet* (Plate 63), was done when de Tonnancour was only twenty-six ; this picture certainly reveals a remarkable nervous grace and precision of drawing as well as an ability to use colour. He has, however, changed his style considerably in recent years. He now is concerned more with flat planes of strong colour, and with the conscious deformation of forms and outlines in still lifes and portraits. These he hopes, by forceful arrangements in design, to be able to invest " with an immutable aspect " and " a feeling for timelessness." Through his concern for these problems he has been driven more and more to study the work of Picasso, for in the creations of this brilliant Spaniard, he says, he finds these qualities in high degree. Yet he struggles to absorb what he learns from Picasso, for " Either you swallow an influence," he concludes, " or you are swallowed by it."

Despite his keen and probing awareness of modern European painting, de Tonnancour never studied in France. Except for his one year in Brazil, where it was the impact of Nature rather than art which had the most effect upon him, his life has been spent entirely in Montreal. After finishing secondary school, he passed four desultory and sterile years at the Ecole des Beaux-Arts and then left when he was twenty-five to study under Goodridge Roberts. His awakening took place then, and he has paid his tribute to Roberts in a booklet which he wrote on that painter and which was published in 1944 by Les Editions de l'Arbre in Montreal.

De Tonnancour expresses himself well in both French and English and, like Lyman before him, his influence on his contemporaries, as he grows older, may in time tend to derive as much from his sound affirmations, in print and in speech, of basic æsthetic judgments, as from the force of his painting, no matter how impressive this, too, may turn out to be when he has more completely absorbed what he is trying to learn from Picasso.

As he is a representative of youth in Canadian art, one can do no better than to include in the final pages of this book some excerpts from an essay he wrote recently on the need for a greater humanity in art.

" The inner man," he explained, " being the true centre of painting and of all the arts, should permeate any subject matter. The artist does not necessarily need, as a vehicle for the expression of this, a human face or a human body, although he may find more adequate possibilities in using these. Granted that he has correctly chosen the type of painting which will meet most clearly his needs of expression, he can project himself just as well through the forms of leeks, pears, clouds and trees as through those of Venus. . . . A hidden element of indefinite depth, imbedded in one's inner psychic being, inserts itself between the eye that receives an impression and the hand that transmits the expression. In this subconscious space of the mind, which is so despairingly hard to force open and to deepen, and which academic art so stubbornly refuses to explore, there is found the most precious of all gifts, a feeling for timelessness. . . .

" This gift is not in itself creative, but it is one around which all the actual creative powers in an artist should gravitate.

" Why then is this gift of such rare occurrence in Canadian art ?

" For a moment we must go down to the roots of our art and consider the soil from which it draws its substance. The first Canadians had left behind them a European culture, which had been slowly and simultaneously developed on all planes of life ; in this new land they had to solve all over again those problems which in the older continent had been dealt with centuries before.

" Colonising meant a compulsory bend of the mind towards immediate material problems ; it meant territorial discoveries in quick succession, with a nomadic outlook resulting, and, soon, the development of a civilisation that was, if anything, over-stimulated by its abnormally speedy growth.

" At any rate, the speedier life we have lived in this race with Europe was not and is not really a more thorough and a more intense one. The so-called ' machine age ' or ' century of speed,' for which America at large is in the greater part responsible, and to which she subscribes so passionately, is in fact a time-shrinking machine intended to compensate for the loss of the richer and more slowly matured civilisation and culture of Europe. This time-shrinking machine has also had a *humanity-shrinking* effect on most of us. In trying to astonish and to beat a rival we have fooled ourselves dangerously. Our habit of saving time led us to save it for the sake of saving it ; and this proves to be a wrong preparation for tasks which require time in unlimited quantities.

" I believe that it is more than hypothetical that the deficiencies of our artistic production are intimately bound up with our vitiated concept of time. This would explain to a certain extent why Canadian art falls back so much on fleeting and transitory values, calmly slurring over things essential.

" I repeat it is not a matter of technical ability we are up against, but a matter of understanding what is the source, the essence and the function of art. This implies a widening of our panoramic view on life and a constant search into our inner selves, where the world makes sense beyond and above the purely physical relationships of things and where we can organise a hierarchy of values. Then art would become a mystic experience outgrowing technical and even intellectual considerations and reaching far into spiritual depths.

" On this continent where time is money, it is extremely difficult to develop this attitude. We want quick answers. Approximations, immediate results and all short cuts give us a sufficient pleasure. . . .

" Should this surprise us ? There are no secret reasons why our normal tempo of living should not pervade our artistic approach and have a marked repercussion on it : since we live so much in time, in measurable time, we want our art to be in it too. From then on everything is wrong, however good may be our intentions. . . .

" When André Malraux wrote in his *Psychologie de l'Art* : ' We perceive that the plastic arts are never born out of a way of seeing the world but out of a way of making it,' he meant of making a world autonomous and in the light of eternity, one that is timeless and above the earthly, rational and practical one. A *sur*-reality ! . . .

" Art has nothing to serve and nothing to prove but the transcending existence of. beauty, so recalling man to his spiritual vocation. To quote

Malraux again : ' It finds its end when it tears men away from the human condition and gives them access to the sacred condition.'

" This is why at all times, when art reached its highest levels, it had a static character, a god-like immobility and a most intemporal, religious and saintly mode of life. And the best of contemporary art is no exception to this truth, even if conceived outside of any normally accepted religious subjects and intentions. . . .

" Hope for Canadian art will not dawn upon us from learning how to paint better ; this will be an automatic consequence of developing better integrated human beings, wide enough and deep enough to have an insight into eternity and who will place the aim of their painting, of their sculpture or their architecture at the level of this ' sacred condition,' subordinating everything else to it."

THE END

INDEX